jazz improvisation

in theory and practice

jazz improvisation

in theory and practice

Bruce Benward
University of Wisconsin, Madison
Joan Wildman
University of Wisconsin, Madison

wcb
Wm. C. Brown Publishers
Dubuque, Iowa

wcb group

Wm. C. Brown
Chairman of the Board
Mark C. Falb
*President and Chief
Executive Officer*

Cover photograph from Stock
Photos, Inc.
Section 1 © 1977 Cliff Moore/
TAURUS PHOTOS
Sections 2 and 3 © 1980
Frank Sitemann/TAURUS
PHOTOS

wcb

Wm. C. Brown Publishers, College Division

Lawrence E. Cremer
President
James L. Romig
Vice-President, Product Development
David Wm. Smith
Vice-President, Marketing
David A. Corona
Vice-President, Production and Design
E. F. Jogerst
Vice-President, Cost Analyst
Marcia H. Stout
Marketing Manager
Linda M. Galarowicz
Director of Marketing Research
Marilyn A. Phelps
Manager of Design
William A. Moss
Production Editorial Manager

Book Team

Karen Speerstra
Senior Developmental Editor
Mark E. Christianson
Designer
Natalie Gould
Production Editor
Mary M. Heller
Visual Research Editor
Mavis M. Oeth
Permissions Editor

Consulting Editor
Frederick W. Westphal
California State University, Sacramento

Contents

Section 1 *Basic Improvisation*

v

Section 3 *Advanced Improvisation*

Exercises

Compositions

Preface

Every jazz musician needs to develop not only an awareness and understanding of jazz tradition but a personal style within that tradition. As jazz is introduced in the classroom, however, these two elements sometimes become unnecessarily separated.

Jazz students should not be content to read big band charts but should also be able to contribute improvisations in the nonnotated sections. Neither is it sufficient for jazz students to memorize changes from a number of tunes if their improvisations on these tunes more closely reflect the contents of a scale pattern book than possibilities within the original music. In short, jazz education requires a synthesis of musical tradition and the development of personal style. Without the element of individuality, a formal jazz education will simply produce regurgitated "school music tradition" and not the subtle interplay of traditional concepts and their maturation in a personal style: the interplay that constitutes the true jazz heritage.

Thus, *Jazz Improvisation in Theory and Practice* fuses basic aural and analytical concepts with personal expression through improvisational playing. It is designed to answer the usual pedagogical questions What? and How? and to equip students to answer the questions Why? and Why not? At the end of the course of study, students should not only know what to do and how to do it, but should also have learned to think for themselves and to develop their own personal styles of performance within the general guidelines of jazz improvisation.

The authors wish to thank the following professors who so carefully reviewed their manuscript at various stages:

Jeffrey Haskell
University of Arizona, Tucson

Frederick C. Tillis
University of Massachusetts, Amherst

Henry C. Wolking
University of Utah, Salt Lake City

Allan M. Wright
Shenandoah College, Virginia

How to Use the Book

Although *Jazz Improvisation* is designed for a sequence of three quarters or two semesters, the ideas presented are those basic concepts that will demand attention throughout a jazz musician's playing career.

Organization

The book is arranged in three sections, which correspond to elementary, intermediate, and advanced levels of improvisational playing.

Each section contains materials that focus on aspects of (1) *melodic patterns;* (2) *scale formations;* (3) *chord formations and relationships;* (4) *the interdependence of scales, chords, and keys; and the evolution of structure.* Sections 1 and 2 also contain chapters on *rhythm* (articulation and accent structure in Section 1 and beat placement in Section 2).

Subject	Section 1	Section 2	Section 3
Melodic patterns	Chapter 2	Chapter 8	Chapter 14
Scale formations	Chapter 3	Chapter 9	Chapter 15
Chord formations and relationships	Chapter 4	Chapter 10	Chapter 16
Interdependence of scales, chords, and keys	Chapter 5	Chapter 11	Chapter 17
Evolution of structure	Chapter 6	Chapter 12	Chapter 18
Rhythm and articulation	Chapter 7	Chapter 13	

Thus, depending upon the level of individual students or needs of the class as a whole, the instructor might choose to

1. follow through the text as written, chapter by chapter
2. concentrate on one section at a time, alternating between chapter topics as needed
3. occasionally stress one specific topic from one section to the next (scale formations in chapter 3 might be followed by tetrachord and symmetrical combinations in chapter 9, for example)

Advanced students should always be encouraged to work at the next higher level whenever possible.

Technical Exercises

In addition to the playing assignments throughout the book, which are to be performed in class, twenty-seven technical exercises have been specifically designed to develop individual performance skills during private practice times outside of class. Gradually becoming more complex, these exercises closely relate to the performance concepts throughout sections 1 and 2. (Transposition must be done at sight or by ear: Tetrachord or scale numbers are added to aid the learning process.) From chapter 14 onward (section 3), however, the student is strongly advised to create his or her own exercises in order to establish logical and personal practice routines.

Cassette Tape

The cassette tape recording consists of a quartet (Les Thimmig, saxes; Joan Wildman, piano; Richard Davis, bass; Michael Weiss, drums) performing:
1. Original tune excerpts as melodic, intervallic, and harmonic dictation exercises;
2. ii–V–I melodies and progressions in all keys;
3. ii–V melodies and progressions using all possible root movements;
4. twelve-bar blues melodies and progressions in all keys.

The purpose of the tape recording is to develop aural skills and to develop individual practice routines. Thus, although each student may spend a considerable amount of time working with this material privately, there are also many class assignments listed throughout the text in which the tape is used. The directions and necessary notational information are found in the perforated material in Appendixes III–V.

Smithsonian Collection of Classic Jazz

The recordings in the *Smithsonian Collection* have been used as a companion anthology to many of the assignments and concepts throughout the book.

Summary

Depending on the class needs and the choice of the instructor, *Jazz Improvisation* provides maximum flexibility:

1. The chapters are organized to allow a variety of directions and emphases.
2. The technical exercises, in addition to the playing assignments, provide an ongoing development of skills in each chapter.
3. The cassette tape provides ear training materials as well as further opportunities for developing playing skills.
4. The frequent references to the *Smithsonian Collection of Classic Jazz* locate actual performances throughout the history of the jazz tradition in the most complete and accessible anthology of recorded jazz styles.

jazz
improvisation
in theory and practice

Section 1

Basic Improvisation

The materials in chapters 1 through 7 embrace the categories (chapter titles) that are basic to the development of improvisational concepts and skills. Although you must pursue one category at a time, it is important to begin to look for connections between one category and another. You must be able to concentrate on keeping the time, for instance, while playing the chord changes and/or a melodic improvisation over the twelve-bar blues.

Introduction

1

The education of a musician in the jazz curriculum at a college or university level parallels that of other music majors in most respects. Only a few differences exist. Of the basic musical elements (pitch, duration, timbre, and intensity) courses taken by all music students will have emphasized pitch relationships. But, while improvisatory performance requires a successful combination of all musical elements, duration (time) is the backbone of all jazz performance and requires intensive study. Indeed, duration (including time in general and rhythm in particular) must occupy a major portion of study for the jazz student.

In the European tradition, downbeats are normally stressed, but jazz performers instinctively stress weak beats or weaker portions of beats (beats two and four of 4/4 or the second of two eighth notes).

Listen to various recorded excerpts from different sides of the *Smithsonian Collection,* and clap on the second and fourth beats of each 4/4 measure while listening to the rhythms and accents produced by the shorter durations. If you have difficulty determining where beats two and four are, spend even more time on this important project.

Assignment 1

Notation

Jazz notation does not reflect the upbeat emphasis within the music. Perhaps the most common of all jazz rhythms is the eighth-note pattern ♫ ♫ . Although the written music would seem to indicate notes of equal value, the player usually fluctuates between ⎡3⎤ ♩♪ ⎡3⎤ ♩♪ and ⎡5⎤ ♫♫♫ . (Most musicians tend to approach ♫ ♫ more closely as the tempo increases.)

The non-notated accents found within the basic rhythmic pattern, although maintaining the superiority of the upbeat, can change from ♫ to ♫ , depending on the pitch relationships and other accents in the phrase. Note also that accents are of varying degrees of loudness. The beginning bars of "Lobsters on Toast" for instance, are shown in figure 1.1: (a) as notated and (b) as might be interpreted by the player.

Figure 1.1

LOBSTERS ON TOAST by Joan Wildman. © 1984 by Joan Wildman.

Note that with repetition of the melodic pattern (at a different beat in the measure) the accents fall on different pitches. Also, even though accents two and five are louder (both occurring on the last note of the pattern), accent five will be the strongest of all because of the need to resolve tension generated throughout the phrase.

"Lobsters on Toast," as with many other jazz tunes and improvised solos, is constructed from very few pitches. Although rhythm is one of the dominant forces, the pitch order and placement in the measure also contribute to that intangible phenomenon in jazz known as *swing*.

Play the "Lobsters on Toast" excerpt, using jazz rhythms (as in version (b) of fig. 1.1), then play the notated melodies below in a jazz style. *It is assumed that the rhythms in all musical examples throughout the book will be interpreted in the jazz style.*

Assignment 2

Repeat several times:

Summary

Jazz performance requires, more than other musical performances, greater attention to duration and its related components. The development of a steady pulse, with idiomatic accents (both in improvisation and in reading notation), is *vital* to the success of any jazz performer.

Summary Activity

Drop the needle on any recording from the *Smithsonian Collection.* Play a repeated pitch (any pitch will do) on beats two and four. After you feel comfortable with the tempo, *turn the volume all the way down, and keep playing.* After a while (as you are continuing to play) turn the volume back up once again. *Are you still playing on beats two and four?*

Melodic Patterns

A melodic pattern consists of any series of pitches used to form a musical unit (from a motive to a phrase). While most melodic patterns span approximately one octave (and often consist of only four or five notes), much melodic variety can be obtained within an even smaller interval span. Figure 2.1 shows the possible five-note choices within a P5, which consist of arrangements of three whole steps and one half step.

Figure 2.1

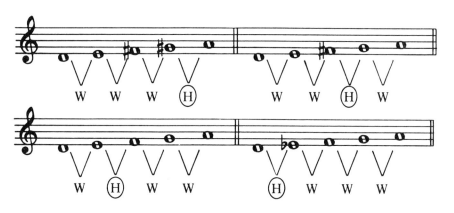

Exercise I

Play the following whole-step and half-step patterns.

Play each segment of figure 2.1. Using only whole notes throughout, no-tice the sharper degree of **tension** between half steps than between whole steps. (Do this carefully. The half step will become the most im-portant interval in your improvisational studies.)Next, play each seg-ment with different note values (alternating half and quarter notes, for example). Listen to the results of longer durations on the tension/re-laxation between pitches.

Construction and Performance

The construction of a melodic pattern requires a careful interaction be-tween pitch and rhythm; neither has to be complex, however. In figure 2.2 the four-bar pattern consists of only three different pitches having only three different durations separated by rests.

Figure 2.2

The performance of a melodic pattern, in order to project a sense of musical coherence, must effect changes of dynamic level and **articulation** (touch) in jazz just as in classical music. However, the jazz player must also "interpret" the notated rhythms, as discussed in chapter 1. Thus, the consecutive eighth notes in figure 2.2 should be played with a triplet feeling and, except for the third grouping in measure 4 (which has a notated accent on the first eighth), it is the *second* eighth of each group which receives the accent.

Play figure 2.2 several times in succession.

Assignment 2

1. Keep a *steady* beat.
2. Insert jazz rhythms and accents.
3. Each accent throughout the line should be louder than its predecessor. (Begin the line's repetition with softer accents and repeat the same procedure.)
4. Play until the melodic pattern functions as a musical unit.

Repetition and Transposition

After the construction and performance of a melodic pattern, the next step is to explore ways of using it in a larger musical context. Probably the most basic methods of enlarging its role is either to repeat the pattern, as in Assignment 2, or play it at another pitch level.

    The transposition of a melodic pattern is not only a means of expanding melodic form, but also functions as a basic vehicle for the coordination of the player with his or her instrument as the player gains an expanded knowledge of musical material.

Assignment 3

Play figure 2.2 up by half steps until you return to the original pitch level. Keep the whole-step-plus-half-step melodic construction in mind.

Pattern Combinations

The combination of melodic patterns can be used simultaneously, alternated, repeated, placed at new pitch levels, or used as a basis for improvisation. Figure 2.3 depicts a five-note pitch pattern from which three short melodic patterns are constructed. Because of the overlap between patterns, the tension (unrest) and relaxation (repose) of each individual line must be heard both horizontally (melodically) and vertically (harmonically) with idiomatic placement of rhythmic accents.

Figure 2.3

Play figure 2.3, allotting instruments to the same general registers as given in figure 2.3. Listen for consonance, dissonance, and accents. After each individual line sounds unified, take turns adding your own melodic patterns. Other suggestions:

1. Alternate playing melodic pattern 1 between its original pitch level and that of a P4th higher. Take turns improvising one or two patterns above pattern 1 (constructed from some or all the same pitches).
2. Repeat the new melodic patterns until you can hear all the parts at the same time.
3. While two or three melodic patterns are being played, take turns (using the same pitches) improvising a melodic pattern that lasts for four measures. Constantly keep in mind the *unity* of your musical idea, which has been stressed throughout this chapter.

Charles Mingus, one of the foremost jazz innovators in the past few decades, often played repeated melodic patterns, superimposed others, sometimes added a solo line on top, and then alternated between repeated patterns. Listen to "Boogie Stop Shuffle" (*Mingus Ah Um,* Columbia GS8171). The bass line from this tune is notated in figure 2.4.

Figure 2.4

BOOGIE STOP SHUFFLE by Charles Mingus. Copyright by Jazz Workshop, Inc., used by permission.

Assignment 5	Devise at least two melodic patterns of your own, each of which can be repeated. Include some melodic skips. Next, superimpose two other melodic patterns that can be inserted or sometimes deleted during the performance. (Copy one of Mingus's lines from the record.) Add a soloist who can play an eight-measure unified statement. Perform your arrangement in class.
Assignment 6	Listen to the recordings by Count Basie of "Lester Leaps In" (*Smithsonian* 6:1) and by Charles Mingus of "Hora Decubitus" (*Smithsonian* 10:5). Notice the uses of repetition, transposition, and the combinations of melodic lines. Cite another such example from the *Smithsonian Collection*.
Assignment 7	From the accompanying cassette tape, notate Melodic Dictation A and Interval Dictation 1. (Instructions and the required notation are found in Appendix III, pp. 197–98).

Summary

Both variety and interest can be sustained by melodic patterns containing only a few pitches within a small intervallic span and simple rhythmic structure. Through the use of repetition, transposition, and the combination of one pattern with another, linear (melodic) development as well as vertical (harmonic) texture can be explored in fresh, new ways.

Summary Activity

1. With a given starting pitch, a designated class member will improvise a melodic pattern of three or four pitches within one 4/4 measure (paying careful attention to accents within the meter). The rest of the class will "Follow the Leader" by playing the same pattern during the next measure. (If the class does not play accurately, the leader must repeat the same pattern; otherwise, a new pattern will be presented within the next four beats.) Continue (indicated by the symbol ⌇⌇) until the class wishes to change either the leader or the starting pitch.
2. Repeat the first activity, but make the answer or response twice as long—first repeated and then transposed (in the next measure) a half step higher or lower. (Experiment with other transpositions whenever possible.) *Keep the beat!*

(a)

(b)

(half step higher)

Scale Formations

3

Scale types are traditionally introduced by identifying the position of half steps within an octave. The student of improvisation, however, must have not only an instant working knowledge of each pitch relationship within the scale, but must also be able to alter scale degrees at will and combine different scales. Since beginning improvisers are advised to limit themselves to only a few scale pitches at a time, this chapter will begin with a smaller unit—the **tetrachord.**

Tetrachord Relationships

A microcosm of tension/relaxation opportunities, the tetrachord not only serves the beginning improviser, but is a tool for the professional player as well. Furthermore, the combination of tetrachords to form one scale and the combination of tetrachords from different scales provide almost inexhaustible sources of melodic material. Let us begin, however, at a more basic level: *A tetrachord is a series of four pitches that consist of adjacent alphabetical letter names.*

In Exercises II and III, we will label both the first and second tetrachords by the occurrence of the half step. Thus a 3–4 tetrachord is a tetrachord with half steps between the third and fourth degrees (all other intervals are whole steps).

Exercise II

Play the following tetrachords as notated, and then play by ascending half steps.

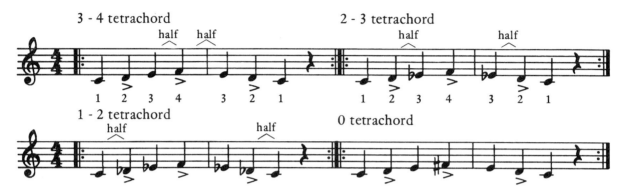

Exercise III

Play the following, and continue each by half steps. (Memorize each pattern.)

Note that the numbers in each example remain constant (i.e., 1–2–3–4–1–2–3–4–3–2–1–1–2–3–4–3–2–1). *Pay careful attention to rhythm and accents—make it swing!*

(c) 1 - 2 tetrachords

(d) 0 tetrachords

Play "Follow the Leader."   **Assignment 1**

1. Choose a pitch.
2. A designated student leader will play a tetrachord (1–2, 2–3, 3–4, or 0) either ascending or descending (quarter notes).
3. After four beats silence, the class will play the same tetrachord (see following example).

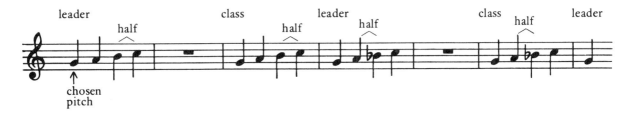

The tetrachords discussed in Exercises II and III can be combined to form scales as follows:

1st Tetrachord	+	2nd Tetrachord	= Scale
3–4	+	3–4	= Major
3–4	+	2–3	= Mixolydian
2–3	+	3–4	= Melodic Minor
2–3	+	2–3	= Dorian
2–3	+	1–2	= Natural Minor
1–2	+	1–2	= Phrygian
0	+	3–4	= Lydian

The notation of these relationships is shown in Exercise IV.

Exercise IV

Play the following tetrachord combinations (scales) a perfect 5th apart (continue each by ascending half steps).

(a) **3 - 4 + 3 - 4** (major scale)

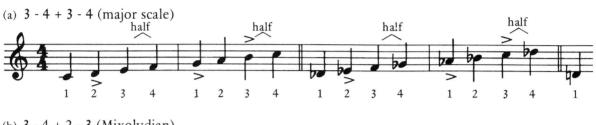

(b) **3 - 4 + 2 - 3** (Mixolydian)

(c) **2 - 3 + 3 - 4** (melodic minor)

(d) **2 - 3 + 2 - 3** (Dorian)

(e) **2 - 3 + 1 - 2** (natural minor or Aeolian)

(f) 1 - 2 + 1 - 2 (Phrygian)

(g) 0 + 3 - 4 (Lydian)

Up to this point, scales have been viewed as formations derived from two specific tetrachords. The next step is to recognize the different tetrachord possibilities of a given seven-note scale unit. For example, pitches 1,2,3,4 or 5,6,7,8 from a major scale can be rethought as 2,3,4,5 and 6,7,8(1),2. The scale remains constant, but its inner relationships change.

Tetrachords within a scale must be heard as a half-step and whole-step microcosm as before, but must now be expanded to include the possibilities found in a seven-note scale.

Play all the major scales as shown in Exercise V.

Exercise V
Play all the major scales as shown. Proceed by ascending half steps: D♭ major, D major, etc.

Assignment 2
Choose a scale to play in the following manner: 1,2,3,4; 2,3,4,5; 3,4,5,6; 4,5,6,7, etc. Focus your listening activities on the sound of each tetrachord as it is being played, as well as on the complete "scale sound" as one tetrachord evolves into the next. For example, if you choose to play D Dorian, listen to the contrasts between the pitch A as you hear it in the tetrachord F,G,A,B (3,4,5,6 of the mode), its appearance as A,B,C,D (5,6,7,1), and its function as the dominant of the scale as a whole: D,E,F,G,A,B,C,D. Now, work with a descending scale in the same way.

Assignment 3
Listen to "Struttin' With Some Barbeque" recorded by Louis Armstrong (*Smithsonian* 2:5). Armstrong's descending pitches from a high (concert) B♭ find several different focal points as he inevitably cascades down the lower octave. Can you hear *different* scales in his melodic pattern despite his beginning each phrase on B♭? Play the first two phrases along with the record until all the notes (and accents) are correct.

Scale Relationships

Obviously, many scales can be constructed from the same tonic pitch, each requiring a different key signature—a Mixolydian mode built on G will have a different key signature from G Phrygian, for example. But then, scales that can be constructed from different pitches using the *same* key signature can also provide a different network of tension/relaxation. For example, since the **major** scale contains **Dorian, Phrygian, Lydian, Mixolydian, Aeolian,** and **Locrian** modes, possibilities are opened for the improviser. The four melodies in figure 3.1, for instance, employ the same key signature (one flat). The first melody begins and ends on F, centers upon the same note, and is therefore in the key of F major. The second melody with its tonal center on G is a Dorian mode melody. The third melody, by the same reasoning, has the character of the Phrygian mode (on A). The fourth melody is in the Lydian mode (on B♭).

Each key and mode in figure 3.1 has its *own* characteristic sound. The special nature of each key or mode is due to (1) the types of tetrachords produced, and (2) the note of repose—the tonal center. Thus, the improviser may have seven scale pitches that can be rearranged to promote seven *different* tonal centers.

Figure 3.1

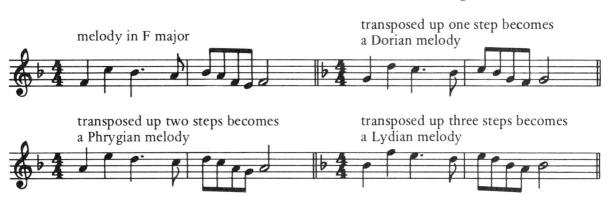

Assignment 4

Play the pitches of each major scale, Dorian mode, Phrygian mode, etc., from the same key signature (i.e., C major: c,d,e,f,g,a,b,c; Dorian mode: d,e,f,g,a,b,c,d; Phrygian mode: e,f,g,a,b,c,d,e; etc.) until you've worked your way back to C major.

Key Relationships

The relationship between keys and their key signatures is shown in the **Circle of Fourths** diagram (fig. 3.2). Although you may have learned the same concept in traditional theory as the "Circle of Fifths," the jazz musician is constantly working in fourths, both with chord relationships as well as key relationships. Moreover, in an improvisation, the player is constantly striving for a target or resolution chord. The "Circle of Fifths" concept, conversely, portrays a sense of movement toward *tension,* ascending a fifth higher toward the dominant (I to V).

Figure 3.2

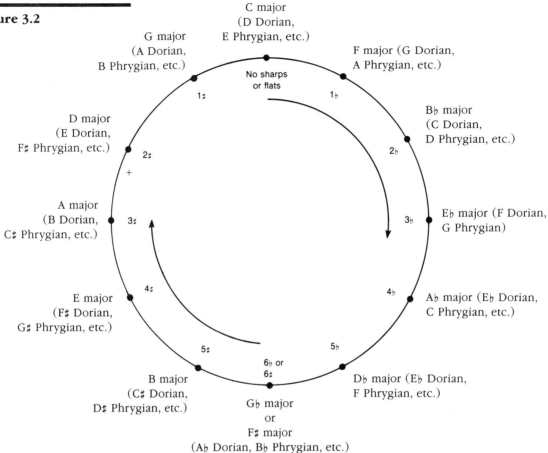

Exercise VI
Play the following scales around the Circle of Fourths (1–1 Major, 1–1 Dorian, 1–1 Phrygian, etc.). Continue with F major and modes containing a key signature of one flat, etc.

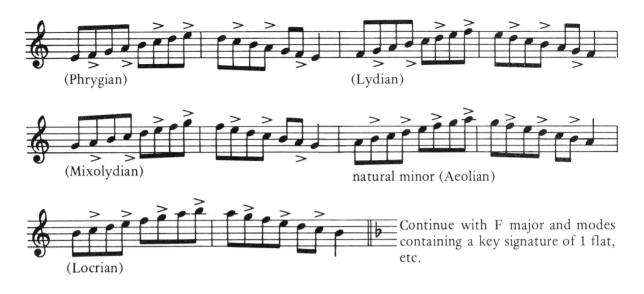

(Phrygian)   (Lydian)

(Mixolydian)   natural minor (Aeolian)

(Locrian)   Continue with F major and modes
                                 containing a key signature of 1 flat,
                                 etc.

Play major scales and modes around the circle (C major, F major, B♭ major, **Assignment 6**
etc.).

Summary

The joining of two tetrachords comprised of half-step and whole-step combinations produces most of our familiar scales. Each scale's quality, however, depends on the tension/relaxation tendencies of its half steps, one of which is usually present within each tetrachord. Thus, a tetrachord is a microcosm that must be fully explored prior to the examination of the completed scale.

Possible seven-note scale formations must next be analyzed, then expanded to include the relationships between scales containing the same key signature. In this instance, despite the different tonal centers and tetrachord organization, the characteristic *sound* of each mode/scale must be retained.

Finally, the relationship between key signatures is exhibited through the Circle of Fourths. Each key a P4th higher adds one flat to its key signature.

Summary Activity

Follow the Leader:

1. On designated pitch, the leader plays any tetrachord ascending.
   The class plays the same tetrachord descending.

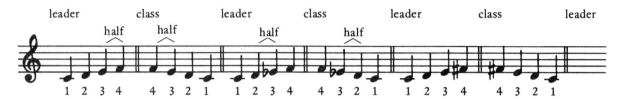

2. On designated pitch, the leader plays any tetrachord ascending or
   descending. The class plays the same tetrachord in the same
   direction one whole step away.
   Optional: Play each scale together after every call-response
   pattern.

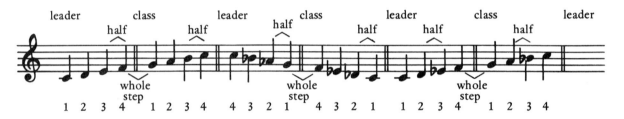

3. On designated pitch, the leader plays any scale ascending or
   descending. The class plays the same scale in the same direction.
   Optional: Play each scale together around the Circle of Fourths.

Chord Formations and Relationships: The Blues

4

All triads and seventh chords are built from various sizes of thirds and sevenths above a given pitch—the root of the chord (fig. 4.1). Although you may have worked with these structures in the past (in a paper-and-pencil setting), you must now be prepared to demonstrate these concepts through the use of your instrument.

Figure 4.1

Chord Construction

The theoretical knowledge of chord construction is only the background information used to develop a working harmonic vocabulary. Just as a thorough understanding of scale function requires the analysis of smaller pitch units, so does harmonic understanding imply an awareness of single pitches in a chord as well as its overall sonority.

Exercise VII

Play (a), (b), (c), and (d) by ascending half steps and then by ascending perfect fourths.

Play (e), (f), (g), and (h) in succession at the same pitch level. Then play each seventh chord type by ascending half steps and next by ascending fourths.

(a) major triad

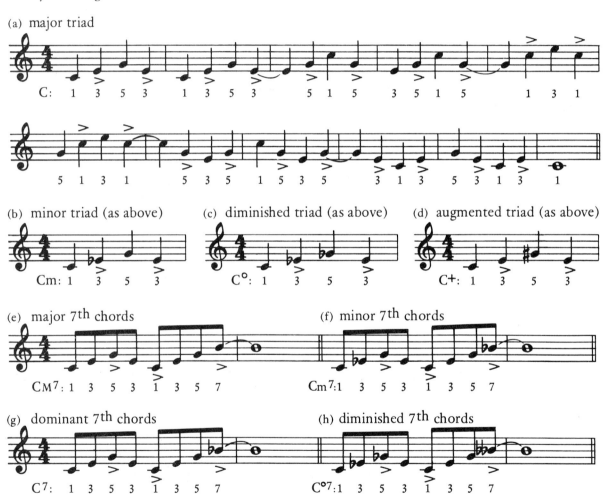

(b) minor triad (as above) (c) diminished triad (as above) (d) augmented triad (as above)

(e) major 7th chords (f) minor 7th chords

(g) dominant 7th chords (h) diminished 7th chords

Play the following pattern illustrating a major triad that develops from a given pitch to an ascending major third and perfect fifth. After playing the pattern in unison (while concentrating on the melodic intervals), play it as a four-part **canon** (each part continued for eight measures), so that the major sound becomes familiar.

  Continue the pattern, building major triads on roots in ascending P4ths. Start with the C major triad, then progress to the F major triad, and continue through B♭, B♭, A♭, etc., in ascending fourths. Next, repeat the pattern, adding the seventh of various chords.

  This assignment demonstrates the *sound* of each chord pitch, in relation to the others, both horizontally and vertically. At first, listen in only one direction; i.e., sort out relationships as they occur either horizontally or vertically. Then, try to hear both horizontal and vertical directions at the same time.

Assignment 1

Chord Relationships

The function of a chord depends upon the placement of the chord root and its members within a specific key. Although a seventh chord can be constructed on each pitch of a scale, and while its quality is acquired by the superimposition of thirds derived from a specific scale, each chord maintains its individual function through the relationship of its root to the tonic (fig. 4.2).

Figure 4.2

C major

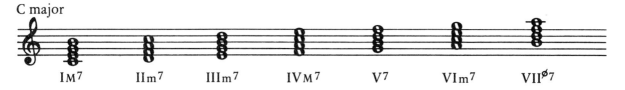

IM7   IIm7   IIIm7   IVM7   V7   VIm7   VII∅7

The tonic is the only chord of a key strong enough to pull all other diatonic chords into a subservient harmonic relationship; even the dominant with its high degree of tension also carries with it the expectation of a succeeding tonic. Since all music moves either *toward* tension or *away* from it, chord progressions are directed toward either the tonic or the dominant. Thus, the strongest tension/relaxation progression is V7/I; ultimately, all other progressions serve only these two chords.

The basic chord functions within a key, (1) tonic and (2) dominant, might be expanded to include (3) the function of **traveling chords** en route to either tonic or dominant. (Traveling chords become especially significant when they progress toward temporary tonics or dominants rather than the expected tonic or dominant of the original key.)

Diatonic Chord Possibilities in a Major Key — Function

Roman Numeral	Scale Degree	Chord Symbol (C M)	Tonic	Dominant	Traveling Chord
IM7	1,3,5,7	CM7	X		
IIm7	2,4,6,8	Dm7			X
IIIm7	3,5,7,2	Em7	(X)		X
IVM7	4,6,8,3	FM7			X
V7	5,7,2,4	G7		X	
VIm7	6,8,3,5	Am7	(X)		X
VII∅7	7,2,4,6	B∅7		X	

Exercise VIII
Play (a) and (b) in all major keys.

Assignment 2

In each major key play

1. the diatonic triads (1,3,5; 2,4,6; etc.)
2. the diatonic seventh chords (1,3,5,7; 2,4,6,8; 3,5,7,2; etc.)

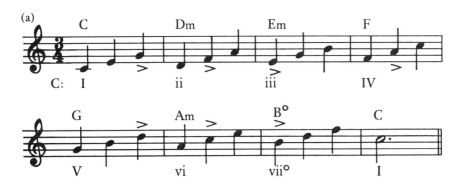

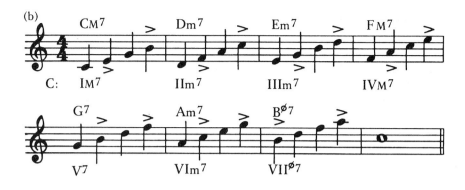

Chord Progressions

When choosing chord progressions, the whole musical unit—a phrase or longer section—must be taken into consideration. The chord-to-chord progression is important, of course, but every phrase must have a high point of tension, and the fluctuation between tension and relaxation within each phrase and section must be carefully calculated.

Also, certain conventional root movements have emerged throughout the history of functional harmony. Sometimes these root movements occur within a single progression, but more often the pattern extends to two or more progressions, and repeated patterns of four or five chords are not uncommon. Listed below are root movement possibilities in order of the frequency of their appearance:

Circle Progression (Ascending P4)   Undoubtedly the most common and the strongest of all harmonic progressions, this progression has the capability, more than any other, to determine a tonality, to give direction and thrust, and to provide order in a section or phrase of music. It is indeed the basis of all harmonic progression.

Some tunes consist almost entirely of circle progressions. Examples: "Lazy River," "Sweet Georgia Brown," "Tune Up," and "Daahoud."

Descending Third   Chord roots that lie in a descending third relationship provide contrast to the more typical ascending fourth relationship, but also act as a shift to convert from one ascending fourth relationship to another or to delay the journey toward the dominant. Examples: "rhythm changes" tunes or traditional thirty-two-bar constructions such as "Don't Get Around Much Anymore."

Ascending Third   Less typical because of the weakening of the tonal center, but useful when this effect is desired. Examples: "Giant Steps" or "All of Me."

Ascending Fifth   The most frequent application is from the tonic to the dominant, providing a feeling of tension or instability and moving away from a tonic. Examples: "Dolphin Dance" or "Bye-Ya."

Ascending Major Second   This progression exemplifies the superimposition of two ascending fifth progressions (C-G-D = C-D). Examples: "Take the 'A' Train," "Mood Indigo." (Ascending M2nds include "Epistrophy," "You Stepped Out of a Dream," and "Well You Needn't.")

Descending Major Second   Only a very small percentage of progressions are of the descending second pattern, although it functions well as a shifting point between ascending fourth patterns. Examples: "Forest Flower" and "Chelsea Bridge." (Descending minor seconds are found in "Pent-Up House" and "Meditation.")

Chord Relationships: The Twelve-Bar Blues

The harmonic relationships in the twelve-bar **blues** graphically illustrate tension and relaxation in a progression of chords. Since the blues originated as a vocal medium, the blues lyrics help define functions of chords within the progression as well as their relationships within the overall form or structure.

Blues lyrics are divided into three sections of four measures each: (1) *relaxation*—the establishment of a mood around which the completed idea will be reflected (I); (2) *growth of tension*—the repetition of the same material to provide emphasis (IV-I); and (3) *tension peak*—the completion of the idea with a statement or "punch line" that brings the problem into focus (V-I). The relationships between the lyrics and the chord progression are shown in "Grayson Street Blues" (fig. 4.3).

Figure 4.3

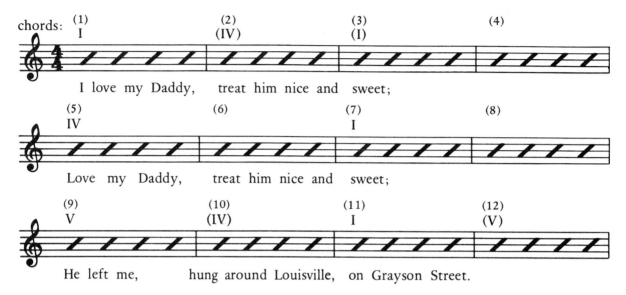

GRAYSON STREET BLUES

Assignment 3   Play the blues progression in figure 4.3 on *piano* (regardless of your major instrument). Memorize the progression and play in two different keys.

Exercise IX
Play the following blues progression on piano until memorized.

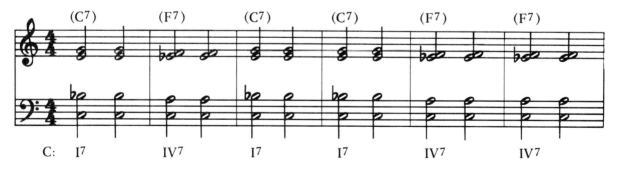

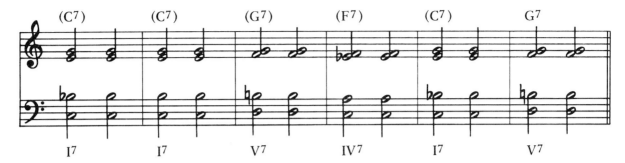

While the basic blues progression complements the vocal message, a more subtle commentary is also provided by the instrumental accompaniment. Note that after each line of lyrics in figure 4.3 there is at least a measure before a new lyric line is presented. The instrumentalist uses these measures, not only to reiterate what has been stated, but also to anticipate the next event, thus providing extra harmonic tension in measures 4, 8, and 12. Indeed the history of jazz harmony might well be capsulized by observing the instrumental treatment of measures 4, 8, and 12 from the early days of the blues down to the present time. (Several of these developments are shown in Appendix V under "Alternate Blues Progressions.")

On Side 1 of the *Smithsonian Collection,* listen to nos. 3,4,5,6 and 8. Try to hear the vocal and instrumental interaction on these cuts. Notice the increase of tension in measures 4, 8, and 12.   **Assignment 4**

Play the blues progression on piano in two new keys: play one chord per measure except in measures 4, 8, and 12. (In those measures play one chord per beat.)   **Assignment 5**

It has often been stated that the jazz musician's first course of study should center upon the blues. This does not mean that it is sufficient to memorize the twelve-bar progression and a few melodic clichés that can be placed haphazardly throughout the progression. It *does* mean that one must listen to the vocal and instrumental interactions of the earliest performers (as well as to contemporary players) in order better to appreciate the tension/relaxation structure of the original form. Only from this understanding can one begin to build a coherent and meaningful improvisation.

We will now attempt to put together some of the ideas discussed thus far as we examine a blues solo excerpt (from "Bag's Groove") recorded by Thelonious Monk (*Smithsonian* 10:1) in figure 4.4.

Figure 4.4

BAG'S GROOVE by Miles Davis. Copyright 1958 Wemar Music Corporation. Reprinted by permission.

Several points described in earlier chapters will be reemphasized here: (1) the rhythmic emphasis on the upbeat, (2) the pitch economy—Monk uses only a two-note melodic pattern throughout the first seven measures, and (3) the relationship between rhythms and pitches which requires careful accent organization. (Review fig. 1.1 and Assignment 1 of chapter 2 for a discussion of accent placement and half-step tension.)

Assignment 6

Play Monk's blues chorus (fig. 4.4) in class *before* you listen to the recording, then play along with his first chorus on the record. Play until your attacks and releases exactly match his.

The two pitches which Monk chose to use at the beginning of his solo function as a dominant (C) ascending a P4 to the tonic (F) in the key of F. Keeping this relationship in mind, play these same twelve bars up by half steps until you return to the original key.

Listen to the rest of his solo. Try to hear the structure of the blues progression at the same time you listen to what he is playing as a soloist. (Note that the progression is not given in the transcription excerpt.) Using Monk's first chorus as your first twelve bars, improvise another chorus, restricting yourself to the following: (1) concentrate on developing what Monk has already begun through your choices of accent patterns; (2) limit yourself, at first, to C,D,Eb,F,Gb. Learn to control these pitches *only;* much more will be discussed about these possibilities later.

Using the accompanying cassette tape, play the twelve-bar blues progression in all keys (notation in Appendix V). First, play the chord progressions on piano as triads; then, using your major instrument, play through the recording again while you improvise upon selected chord tones.

Assignment 7

Summary

All triads and seventh chords are built from various sizes of thirds and sevenths above a chord root. The function of a specific chord depends upon its placement within a key. All diatonic chords function as (1) tonic, (2) dominant, or (3) traveling chords within a progression. The tonic serves as the most relaxed chord of the key; the dominant is the most active; and traveling chords progress toward either tonic or dominant. The twelve-bar blues is a good example of the tension and relaxation inherent in a chord progression.

Summary Activity

Listen to Louis Armstrong's performance of "West End Blues" (*Smithsonian* 2:9). Record the example on tape, then play with the tape to become familiar with the tempo, key, chord progression, etc.

The beginning of the head (after the introduction) is notated in the following excerpt. Transcribe the rest of the twelve bars and play them together in class with the record.

The Interdependence of Scales, Chords, and Keys

5

Harmony and Melody

Melodies and chords are basic tools of the improviser, and their effective combination allows individuals to develop their own musical styles. While melody and harmony are both derived from scales, melody represents linear relationships while harmony produces vertical (sounding together) associations. Thus, in a successful improvisation, it is necessary for both facets of the music to be carefully coordinated.

In both harmony and melody the creation of tension and relaxation is produced in the same manner. For instance, the dominant G (key of C major) projects the same need to resolve to the tonic whether it appears as a note of the melody or as the root of a V7 chord. Similarly, the second scale step D can entail both the traveling function of the ii triad and the movement toward G in a melody.

The linear aspects of melody and the verticality of chords can also be expressed through an interchange of the two. That is, the vertical essence of a chord can be expressed horizontally as a melody. Figure 5.1 shows the IIm7, V7, and IM7 chords displayed as parts of three scales. The horizontal spelling of the IIm7 chord (white notes) produces the scale (melodic) pitches that embody the traveling function of IIm7 in C major. By filling in the remaining notes (white keys) using the pitches of the C major scale, it is apparent that the Dorian mode best illustrates the qualities inherent in the IIm7 chord sonority. Similarly, the dominant seventh chord (V7) is represented by the Mixolydian mode while the IM7 is suggested by the C major scale itself.

Figure 5.1

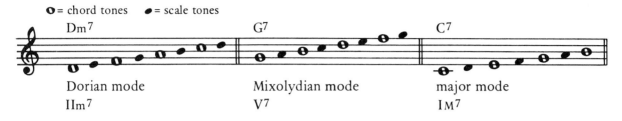

Assignment 1

From the following chords and key signatures, write the scales that most closely reflect each chordal function. Identify each scale, key, and diatonic function of the chord (I, ii, iii, IV, V, vi, vii°).

Illustration

chord: IM⁷

mode: major

key: C major

1.   scale:

2.

3.

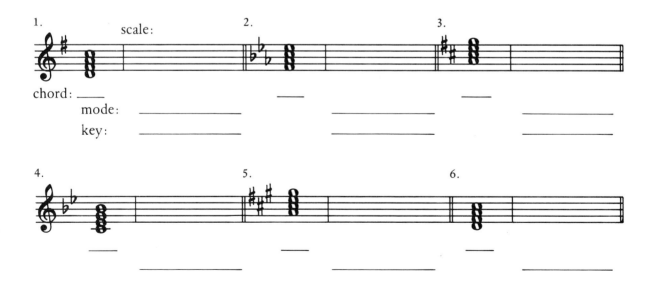

chord: _____

mode: _____

key: _____

4.

5.

6.

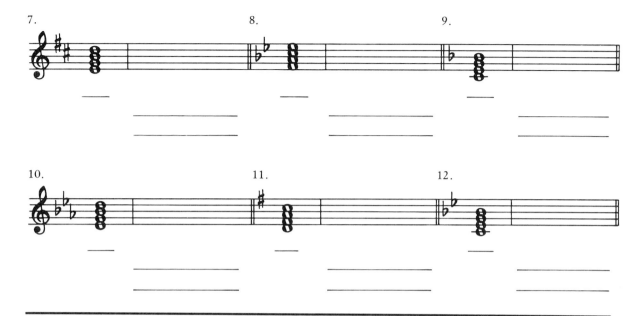

Harmony, Melody, and Key

Both horizontal and vertical functions are implied in the relationship between chords and melodies, although those same functions are enlarged upon when different chords are connected. As a chord progression symbolizes a journey toward a key center (whether completed or not), chordal and scalar material must reflect the distinguishing aspects of the expected tonic. For example, although the D Dorian and G Mixolydian modes represent the scales used for the ii–V progression in C major, the overriding presence of C is indicated since all its scale pitches are contained in both D Dorian and G Mixolydian modes. Thus, a ii–V–I progression contains only the pitches of the tonic scale.

Exercise X

Play the following scales and
chords around the Circle of
Fourths.

(a) Scale and chords (Dm7
and so on to B♭)

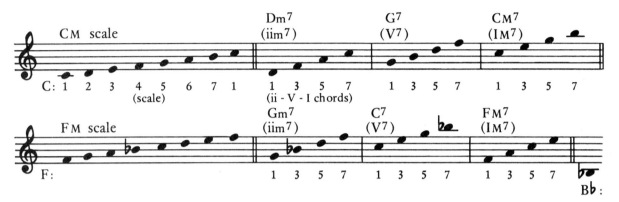

(b) Chords (1–7–5–3)

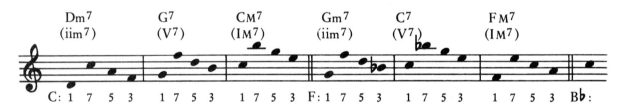

(c) Chords (7–5–3–1)

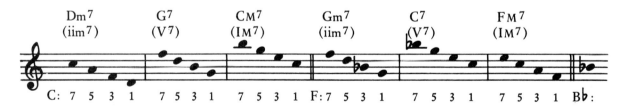

(d) Continue with 1–7–3–5;
7–1–3–5; 5–1–7–3;
3–1–5–7; etc., of each ii,
V, and I chord as
desired.

Play the scale/chord relationships around the Circle of Fourths (harmonic notation for the entire Circle is listed in Appendix IV). First play the two preliminary exercises, then use the accompanying cassette recording of the ii–V–I progression.

Assignment 2

Preliminary Exercises

Play with the ii–V–I recording

Scales and Chords in Transitory Keys

Often the arrival of a new tonic will be frustrated in mid-progression by the suggestion of a new, different tonal center. For example, after hearing a ii–V of one key, the harmony might suddenly shift to a ii–V–(I) of another key. This process of avoiding the expected tonic not only prolongs the existing tension of the V chord but *increases* it through the change of direction.

The effective use of transitory keys can unlock possibilities for new structural shapes on both the microlevel and macrolevel. Not only does the alteration of expected harmonies sustain higher tension levels for a longer period of time, as suggested earlier, but it also forecasts melodic and rhythmic innovations which can affect the overall structure of a tune.

The insertion of a nondiatonic ii–V to promote a transitory key feeling can occur within any key relationship, depending upon the desired shape of the music. When writing a composition, for example, one is guided only by self-imposed structural limitations; whereas, in an improvisation of given material the ii–V insertions are governed by the external structure of the tune. Figure 5.2 illustrates various key relationships that can be implied by added ii–V's (ii–V insertions are circled) both singly and in combination.

Figure 5.2

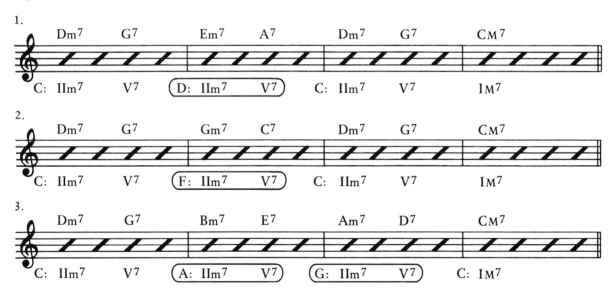

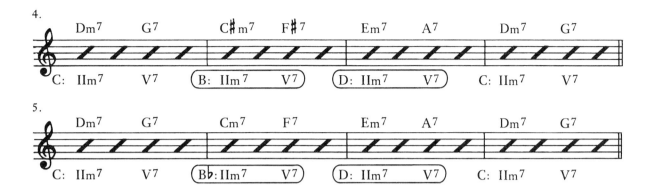

While the progressions in figure 5.2 all contain four measures of C major with added ii–v's from other keys, note that nos. 1 and 2 resolve to the original tonic while nos. 3, 4, and 5 end on the dominant.

Exercise XI
Play the following around the Circle of Fourths.
(a) No. 1 of figure 5.2

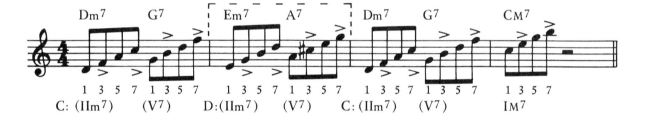

(b) Continue around the Circle. Then play nos. 2–5 of figure 5.2

(c) This example contains a ii–V progression of E♭ between the ii and V of C major. Play around the Circle. Note the chord numbers of the last two chords.

Assignment 3

Write a harmonic progression of two four-measure phrases in the key of Bb major. End the first phrase on the dominant, the second on the tonic, and insert ii–V's as in figure 5.2. (Use different key relationships than those given in fig. 5.2.)

Assignment 4

Using the accompanying recording (ii–V by descending M2nds), play (as shown in the following notation)

    1. 1,3,5,7 of each chord
    2. the Dorian and Mixolydian modes on each ii–V
    3. the melodies performed on the recording.

Assignment 5

From accompanying cassette recording, do Melodic Dictation B and Interval Dictation 2 (notation and instructions in Appendix III).

Assignment 6

Listen to the added ii–V progressions that Don Byas uses in "I Got Rhythm" (*Smithsonian* 7:5). (Note the contrast of the roots of the bassist's chords that are simultaneous with those of the sax player.)

Summary

Both chords and scale pitches correspond to the same tonic, dominant, or traveling function; i.e., in the key of C the pitch G creates tension whether used as a melodic pitch or as the root of the dominant chord. Dominant tension can be prolonged by the addition of ii–V progressions from transitory keys. Thus, a ii–V progression from another key can be inserted within a diatonic ii–V to intensify and lengthen the climactic process.

Summary Activity

From the original chords of "There Will Never Be Another You," which follows, construct a new harmonization that uses added or substitute ii–V harmonies to enhance the original structure. Play in class.

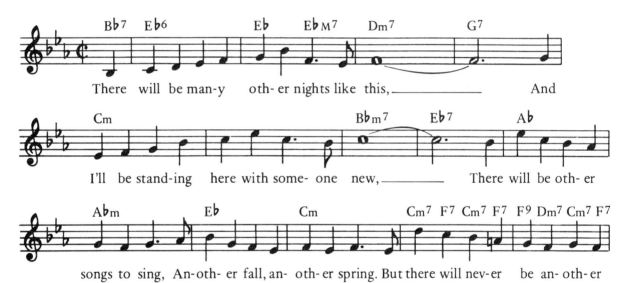

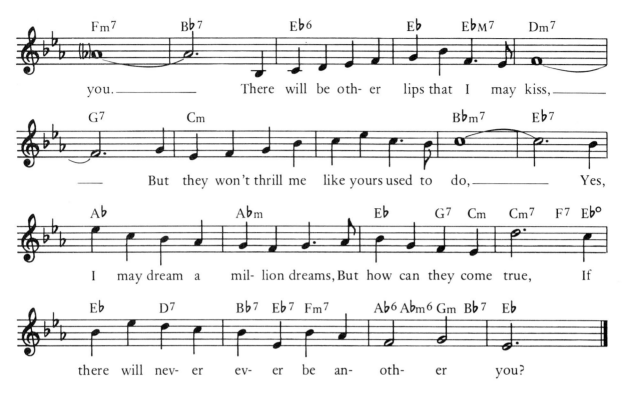

The Evolution of Structure

6

The structure of a jazz composition or its improvisation is built from (1) **motives,** (2) **phrase members,** (3) **phrases,** and (4) **periods,** just as music from the European tradition. In jazz—the American art form—there is often a shift in emphasis, however, as African traditions are combined with European influences.

Motives

Motives often carry remnants from African **call-and-response** patterns in that (1) tension is often derived from repetition rather than from development and (2) there is a tendency for jazz motives to be longer than those from European literature. In figure 6.1, the *soloist* uses a motive that is altered in repetition. The lyrics change as well—suggesting a developmental form. However, the *group* always responds with the same words in the same rhythm—suggesting a repetitive form. In order to construct a coherent statement, the lyrics require both the call and response motives to be longer perhaps than would instrumentally derived motives from the European tradition.

Figure 6.1

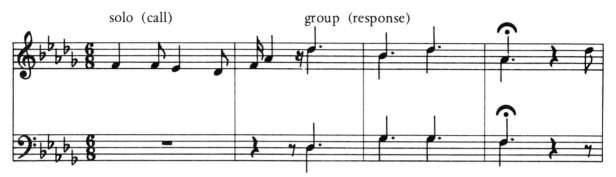

CALL ME HANGIN' JOHNNY. Excerpt from SLAVE SONGS OF THE GEORGIA SEA ISLANDS by Lydia Parrish. Copyright © 1942 by Lydia Parrish, renewed © 1969 by Maxfield Parrish, Jr. Reprinted by permission of Farrar, Straus and Giroux, Inc.

In the following excerpt from the big band era (fig. 6.2), the call-and-response pattern is shown in an abbreviated version: both are congealed into a single motive. The motive is then repeated several times over chord changes to complete an entire section. These repeated motives, called **riffs,** have been used in a variety of musical settings, sometimes behind a soloist or superimposed upon each other (as is demonstrated in "Boogie Stop Shuffle"), thus creating a call-and-response pattern simultaneously.

Figure 6.2

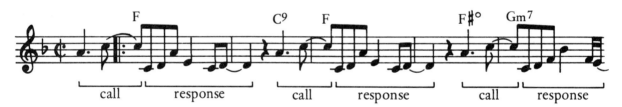

STOMPIN' AT THE SAVOY by Benny Goodman, Chuck Webb, Edgar Sampson, Andy Razaf. © 1936 Robbins Music Corporation. © Renewed 1964 Pic Corp. International Copyright Secured. All Rights Reserved. Used By Permission.

Another example, shown in figure 6.3, is a two-measure motive from a more contemporary tune. It is used for the first eight bars of the composition, this time over a two-chord framework.

Figure 6.3

MERCY, MERCY, MERCY by Josef Zawinul. Copyright Gopam Enterprises, Inc. Reprinted by permission.

Listen to recordings (1) by James P. Johnson of "Carolina Shout" (*Smithsonian* 2:4), (2) by Jimmie Lunceford of "Lunceford Special" (*Smithsonian* 5:3), and (3) by Dexter Gordon of "Bikini" (*Smithsonian* 9:3). Notice James P. Johnson's use of motives that are quite short and of regular lengths. In the early days of jazz piano, much of the formal structure had evolved from European influences, particularly the march, while the motivic rhythm maintained an African influence. Musicians gradually lengthened the motivic structure, with the extensive use of riff patterns (reminiscent of the call and response), by the time of the swing era (the period of Jimmie Lunceford). This "Americanization" of the music continued into the bebop period as we hear the same motive used at the beginning of the first several phrases.

Assignment 1

Phrase Members

A phrase member, (a term applicable to phrases that have easily distinguished elements within them) is a definitive element of a phrase. The first phrase member provides the basic musical information, and the second is a repetition or development of that information.

Phrases in a jazz composition often consist of two phrase members of two to four measures each. The first phrase member might be a repetition of a motive while the second might restate or develop the first phrase member. Figure 6.4 shows the second phrase member as restatement of the first with an added half rest.

Figure 6.4

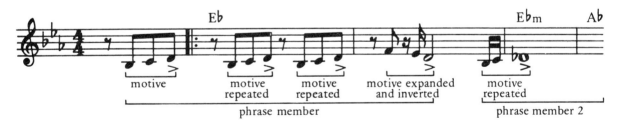

FOUR by Miles Davis. © 1963 Prestige Music. Used by permission.

Ballads tend to consist of longer phrase members (and phrases) than up-tempo tunes. Fast bebop compositions, for example, often comprise motives lasting a measure or less, with unequal durations, including rests within and between divisions. Some well-known tunes are defined according to the length of their phrase member structure. This does not directly relate to tempo—"There Will Never Be Another You," for example, can be played as a ballad or also as up-tempo—only the duration of each segment vis-à-vis the whole form is used as a criterion.

Examples of ballads (longer and more even lengths of construction) are "There Will Never Be Another You," "Summertime," "Solitude," "I Got It Bad," "Round Midnight," "Mood Indigo," "Have You Met Miss Jones," and "What's New."

Up-tempo (shorter or uneven lengths of construction) examples are "Groovin' High," "Move," "Criss Cross," "Thrivin' on a Riff," "Scrapple from the Apple," "Ornithology," "Jordu," "Four," "Daahoud."

Phrases

A phrase is the culmination of smaller units such as motives and phrase members in a dependent or independent musical thought ending with a cadence. Often longer than the traditional four-bar phrase of the European tradition, a beautiful eight-measure phrase by Duke Ellington is demonstrated in figure 6.5.

Figure 6.5

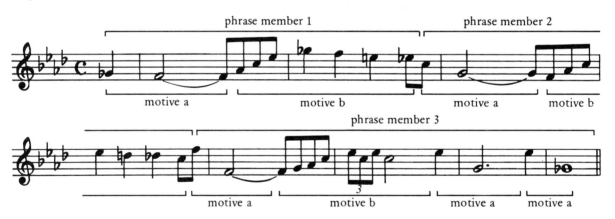

Periods

A period is a combination of two (or more) repeated, parallel, or contrasting phrases. While most jazz compositions exhibit the first conclusive cadence at the end of sixteen bars, temporary modulations also play an important role—sometimes as many as four or more temporary modulations (secondary dominants) within the first eight bars. Such transitory modulations are especially important in phrase connection.

A standard example of a period within an A section (sixteen measures) of a thirty-two-bar composition is given in figure 6.6. The first eight measures are repeated, ending with a conclusive cadence in measure 16.

Figure 6.6

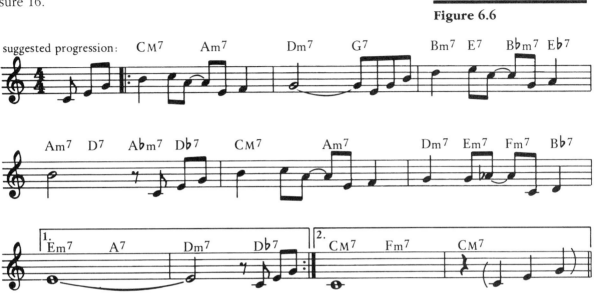

Exercise XII

Play the following phrases on piano (play harmonies in left hand). Continue each phrase around the Circle of Fourths to F, B♭, etc.

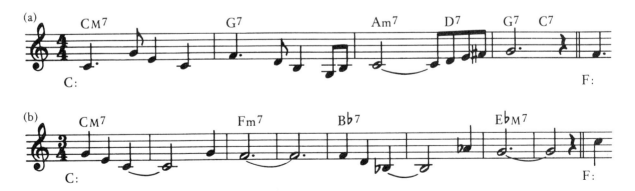

Assignment 2   Write a melodic motive, extend it into a phrase member, and finally into a phrase. Play it in class (no rhythm section) and improvise a parallel or contrasting phrase to comprise a period.

The Overall Form of a Jazz Composition

If the first, or A, period is sixteen bars, the B, or contrasting section, is usually eight bars long followed by an eight-bar repetition of A; thus, a thirty-two-bar composition in all. The following are typical forms found in jazz compositions.

Typical Melody	A Section	B Section	A Section
32-bar	16	8	8
32-bar	12	8	12
24-bar	12	12	–
16-bar	8	8	–

(It must be remembered that many jazz compositions are written also over the twelve-bar blues and in less traditional forms, such as AAB; ABCA; or ABB, for example.)

The most noticeable contrast between the A and B sections is the change of key. While performers often change the rhythmic format between the A and B sections (from a Latin to a swing beat, for instance), the less stable B section can also promote contrast through changes in pitch contours, rhythmic variety, and varied harmonic rhythm.

Figure 6.7 shows sixteen measures from a composition of extraordinary craftsmanship.

Figure 6.7

Listen to "Lady Bird" as recorded by Tadd Dameron (*Smithsonian* 9:2). Play the tune until both its melodic line and chord progression are memorized. Review the topics discussed in this chapter as they relate to this tune:

1. Trace each motive, phrase member, and phrase as it evolves throughout the composition.
2. How is contrast provided between the A and B sections?
3. How do the soloists in the recording observe these contrasts? Give examples of soloists' motives being generated by the chord progression or the given melodic line.

Assignment 3

Write a sixteen-bar tune that could be used as an A section of a thirty-two-bar composition. Play it in class and take turns improvising several choruses.

Assignment 4

Summary

Jazz compositions and their improvisations are constructed from motives, phrase members, phrases, and periods. While the completed form of a composition might vary from twelve to sixty-four measures, most typical lengths are twelve (usually the blues), sixteen, and thirty-two bars in an ABA, AB, ABB, or AAB form.

Summary Activity

Play "fours" as follows:

1. Using the blues progression, each class member in succession will improvise four measures, keeping the progression intact.
   Remember after the third student plays, the next person will start improvising at the top (start) of the form once again. (The blues progression is twelve measures long, and each player improvises on four measures.) Try to incorporate some of the material of the previous player into your own four-measure solo.
2. Trade fours with the drummer: a horn player improvises on the first four measures of the progression, followed by the drummer playing the next four, another horn player completes the form, while the drummer begins the new chorus, etc. Continue playing in this fashion until all class members have had a chance to play several times.
3. Trade "eights" in the manner described for fours, using the tune "Lady Bird," which you have recently learned. Watch the *time* in addition to the form.

Rhythm and Articulation

The most important aspect of jazz performance is the concept of time, and the most fundamental aspect of time is a regular pulse. Ironically, most timekeeping problems are caused by a tendency to reduce pulses into smaller and smaller subdivisions. In order to swing, time must flow naturally from one beat (measure) to another; thus, instead of compressing pulses into rigid micro-units, the player must constantly relate to a larger framework (allowing the smaller units to gravitate naturally toward the next rhythmic goal).

Playing in a Group

Group playing demands not only the perception of time by each individual, but also the awareness of *group time* as produced by all other members simultaneously. Although this seems to be a very simple idea, it is much more difficult to accomplish than one might think.

Assignment 1

From a tempo given by the instructor, play the following exercise together (all class members) at a slow tempo. Aim for the *middle* of each notated downbeat. There must be no conducting, foot-tapping, nodding of heads, etc. (Close your eyes and try to internalize the time. Also, don't try to adjust to someone else's time at the next entrance.)

This exercise, particularly at a *very* slow tempo, will take quite a lot of work. Keep doing it until the class feels the time as a group.

During the process of internalizing the time, your first tendency will be to count 1–2–3–4 to yourself and hope to enter with the other players. *Don't!* You will simply come in ahead of the beat. Instead, make yourself listen to the shape of the measure as *one* unit. Apply this to the concept of tension and relaxation: as you begin to hear measure units you will notice a gradual crescendo of tension as you prepare to play the next beat 1. Of course this tension-crescendo occurs during *silence,* but perhaps that makes it all the more powerful as you begin to lock into your own awareness of meter relationships (see fig. 7.1).

Figure 7.1

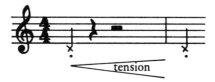

Conceptualizing the measure as *one* unit of time, rather than as four successive quarter-note units, is also preferable to the subdivision of the measure into halves. The limitation of using beats 2 and 4 (or 1 and 3) as basic units becomes apparent as soon as you shift the accent to 1 and 3 (or 2 and 4). Thus, the measure unit not only stabilizes metric regularity but also provides the freedom within that time span for more complex rhythmic possibilities.

While the rest of the class continues to play only beat 1, at a slow tempo, each player in turn should play one note (any pitch, any duration) at any point between the group entrances, which best demonstrates the tension-crescendo toward the next measure. (You are successful if the class enters the next measure at precisely the same time.) See figure 7.2.

Figure 7.2

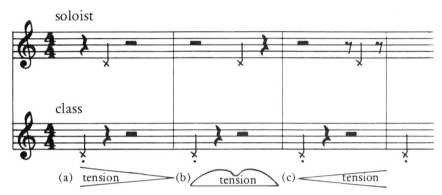

In (a) the soloist enters too soon, before the tension-crescendo has had a chance to begin; (b) breaks the tension-crescendo rather than allowing it to grow throughout the measure; at (c), however, the soloist not only enters at the peak of the crescendo, but also provides more tension since the point of attack does not fall directly on a beat.

Playing as a Rhythm Section

The same result occurs with (a), (b), or (c) in figure 7.2 if a bass player and drummer are added to the group, despite the fact that the walking bass line and the drummer's quarter-plus-eighths necessarily divide the time into smaller units.

Assignment 3

Piano/guitar play a C7 on beat 1 and whatever additional beat is required to play (a), (b), or (c) in figure 7.2. Repeat each measure until you are able to stretch your sense of time across the bar line (instead of becoming "boxed in" by the quarter notes or eighth notes of the bass and drums).

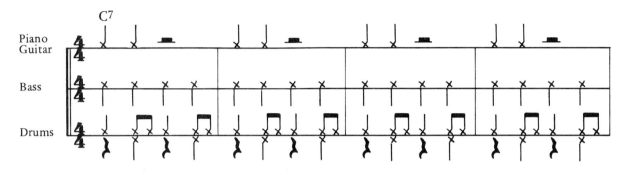

Just as motives and phrases are present in written melodic and solo lines, rhythm section players must also play accompaniment patterns that expand into coherent phrases. Therefore, the tension-crescendo, which presses toward the next measure, is enlarged into a structure of several measures.

Exercise XIII

Play the following rhythms.
(a) Use a metronome to beat *once* during a measure (ca. 0 = 40).

(b) Use a metronome to beat *twice* during a measure (ca. d = 80).

(c) Use a metronome to beat on each quarter (ca. d = 138).

fine

D.C. al fine

Assignment 4   Using the individual rhythms of (a), (b), or (c) of figure 7.2, combine the measures in any order that will make up a four-bar phrase according to the following shape (for example, (c) + (c) + (a) + (a) is not desirable because too much tension is concentrated at the beginning of the phrase):

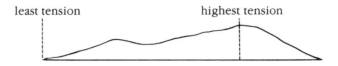

Harmonic rhythm, the relative duration of individual chords within a progression, must also be given structural consideration. In the blues, for example, the larger units to be considered relate to the harmonic changes on I (measures 1–4); IV (measures 5–8); and V (measures 9–12). Whether played by a big-band brass section or a three-piece rhythm section, an accompaniment to the blues has a tendency to be grouped in large rhythmic phrases that correspond to its three-part form.

Assignment 5   As a rhythm section (without soloist), play the blues and set up rhythmic phrases that illuminate the blues structure. Keep it simple—establish only the structure; don't play a solo.

The interaction between rhythm section players, necessary to unify rhythmic phrases or harmonic structures, must be further developed when they **comp** behind (accompany) a soloist. In this instance, the rhythm section players must also react, as a unit, to the soloist's new rhythmic formations, which often contain very short durations or complex motivic configurations. The danger is to *overreact.* When comping behind a soloist who is playing mostly fast notes, the inexperienced player has a tendency to play shorter durations as well, thus complicating the texture and often destroying the soloist's phrase structure. More serious, however, is the tendency to rush the tempo or to play on the wrong side of the beat. Therefore, it seems appropriate to repeat the advice given at the very beginning of the chapter—*relate to larger units of pulse* rather than to their subdivisions.

It is the responsibility of a rhythm section to support a soloist through well-placed accents (not parallel solo lines). Any filler material must be carefully placed to reinforce the soloist's next entrance. Listening to many different types of music can be very helpful in developing this concept. For example, listen to the sounds produced by James P. Johnson's left hand as he comps for his right-hand melody or to Duke Ellington's comping—either behind his band or especially in his small group recordings. It is also useful to listen to classical compositions written for solo instrument or voice with piano accompaniment. Above all, however, practice comping behind your friends' solos.

Playing as a Soloist

All of the above applies to the soloist, but in addition, the solo player must also be concerned with rhythmic aspects at the microlevel. Not only does the soloist usually use shorter durations than does the rhythm section player, but he or she must also relate to their subtle gradations of tension and relaxation.

Temporal relationships on a microlevel really pertain to articulation. Anyone who has heard a nonjazz player read a transcribed Charlie Parker solo and then has compared that performance with the original recording knows the importance of articulation for idiomatic jazz performance. Since jazz articulations have as their basic function the rhythmic thrust toward an eventual downbeat (at either the macrolevel or microlevel), most articulation accents begin on an upbeat as they travel toward their downbeat goal.

Exercise XIV
(a) Play the given pattern using notated articulations.

(b) Play the following repeated patterns in all keys, transposing by ascending half steps.

Assignment 6

Using the accompanying cassette recording (ii–V–I) from Appendix IV, play the following examples around the Circle. Carefully watch the articulation directions.

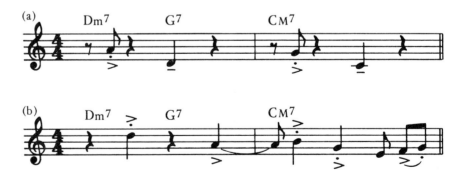

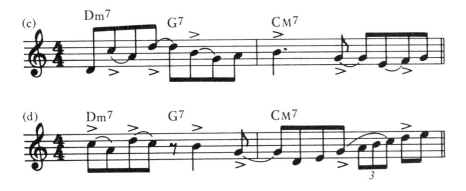

Rhythmic Organization

The notated accents in the articulation exercises of Assignment 6 produce a structural significance of their own. Although jazz accents traditionally fall on the upbeats of a measure, the regularity of upbeat to upbeat accent demands an eventual stress on the downbeat in order to sustain the vitality of the phrase. The process of arranging upbeat/downbeat accents into a higher structural order (providing the strongest swing capabilities) reached its zenith during the bebop period.

   After only a brief acquaintance with the music of Charlie Parker or Thelonious Monk, for example, it is apparent that accent organization can contribute as much to the overall unity of a solo or tune as melodic or harmonic development. This will be demonstrated in figure 7.3 as we trace the development of accent structure throughout the first phrase of Charlie Parker's "Confirmation."

Figure 7.3

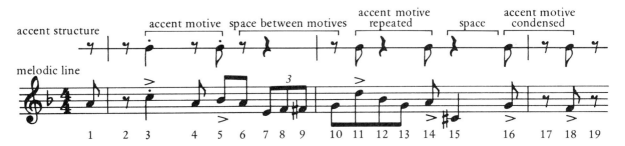

The accents provided by the player are shown above the melodic line. These accents create a structure of their own:

1. Although the pitches change from measure 1 to measure 2, the accents occur at the same places in both measures, setting up an accent motive in measure 1 that is repeated in measure 2.
2. The last two accents (at 16 and 18) restate the accent motive in a compressed form, both in its duration (1 ½ eighth notes) and in the space between entries (the space between the first and second motives is two beats whereas only one beat separates the second and third).
3. This last motivic statement breaks up the "regularity" of the first two versions and, by its condensation, pushes toward the climactic point of the rhythmic phrase at 16.

Assignment 7

Clap the accent structure of figure 7.3. Use dynamics to stress some accents more than others (remember that the peak of the phrase is at 16). Play the first phrase of "Confirmation," and make sure that its accent structure is incorporated into your interpretation.

Assignment 8

Go back to Assignment 6 and play the exercises around the Circle once again, as you relate the articulations discussed earlier to the accent patterns you are now familiar with.

Assignment 9

From the accompanying cassette recording, play the *ascending* M2 progressions from the ii–V series (Appendix IV).

Assignment 10

Listen to the uniformity of accents and articulation played together by Dizzy Gillespie and Charlie Parker at the beginning of "Shaw' Nuff" (*Smithsonian* 7:6). Notice the continuation of the complex rhythmic organization throughout the solos. Contrast the recording with the uniformity of the rhythmic style of a recording made a few years earlier, Lionel Hampton's "When Lights Are Low" (*Smithsonian* 5:6).

Summary

The concept of time in its broadest sense is the most important aspect of jazz performance. The awareness of "group time" implies the ability to think of measure groupings rather than individual beats. This not only stabilizes metric regularity, but also allows freedom within each measure to produce more subtle rhythmic accent-structures.

Rhythm section players must also develop coherent rhythmic structures both individually and as a group. In addition, support must be provided for the soloist's ideas while maintaining the unity of the section.

Although the soloist must be concerned with rhythm on a macrolevel, the relatively shorter durations also demand careful attention at the microlevel. Thus, some of the soloist's primary rhythmic concerns are *articulation* and *accent structure.*

Summary Activity

Review your notation from Melodic Dictations A and B (Appendix III). Play with the tape, exactly matching the phrasing and articulations of the saxophone player.

Section 1 Summary

Chapters 1–7 comprise concepts and activities at an elementary level. The range of these materials are summarized as follows:

Chapter 1. Introduction

Chapter 2. Melodic Patterns Four-note and five-note patterns are examined to discover areas of tension/relaxation, then transposed and/or superimposed onto other melodic groupings.

Chapter 3. Scale Formations Scales are formed by the combination of two tetrachords. Relationships between scales/modes having the same key signature as well as key signature relationships around the Circle of Fourths are described, using *major, minor, Dorian, Phrygian, Lydian, Mixolydian, Aeolian, and Locrian* scales and modes.

Chapter 4. Chord Formations and Relationships: The Blues Diatonic triads and seventh chords are constructed and given a *tonic, dominant,* or *traveling* function within a specific key. Tension/relaxation is discussed in regard to root movements in general, with specific application to the twelve-bar blues.

Chapter 5. The Interdependence of Scales, Chords, and Keys The ii–V–I progressions are equated with Dorian, Mixolydian, and major scales as used in both stationary and transitory keys. Each chord is extended to its unaltered thirteenth through the use of its corresponding scale.

Chapter 6. The Evolution of Structure Both improvisations and jazz compositions are constructed from *motives, phrase members, phrases,* and *periods.*

Chapter 7. Rhythm and Articulation Playing in the *middle* of each beat is discussed from several points of view: playing in a group, playing as a rhythm section, and playing as a soloist. Rhythmic organization is examined from the accent structure of a phrase from ''Confirmation'' by Charlie Parker.

Summary Activity

Transcribe *one* chorus from a solo recorded on either the *Smithsonian Collection* or from one of the albums in the following list. Pick a soloist who plays the same instrument as you do.

1. As discussed in chapter 4, remember to tape your selection, and begin by trying to play along as much as possible to define the tempo, key, progressions, and form.
2. Next, listen to the melodic line many times (without playing), and try to imagine the correct pitches.
3. Play a phrase at a time (without the recording) to see if you were correct.
4. Play along with the record until you can match articulation as well as pitches and rhythms.

Discography

A. Additional anthologies which relate to specific instruments.
   1. *A Jazz Piano Anthology:* Columbia 32355
   2. *The Bass:* Impulse ASY-9284-3
   3. *The Drums:* Impulse ASY-9272-3
   4. *For Horn Players:* The Prestige 24000 Series PRP-1, for instance, includes cuts by Miles Davis, Thelonious Monk, Eric Dolphy, Sonny Rollins, Charlie Parker, and John Coltrane, among others.

B. The Beginnings of Jazz
   1. *Piano Roll Hall of Fame* (includes Jelly Roll Morton, Clarence Williams, Charles Davenport, Thomas "Fats" Waller, Richard M. Jones, James P. Johnson, Steve J. Lewis, Clarence Johnson, Sam Williams, Teddy Weatherfor, Clarence M. Jones, and Jimmy Blythe).
   2. *James P. Johnson (1917–21): Parlor Piano Solos from Rare Piano Rolls.* BLP 1003 Q.
   3. *Eubie Blake Blues and Rags: His Earliest Piano Rolls 1917–1921.* BLP 1011Q Stereo. Vol. 1.
   4. *Ragtime 1: The City (Banjos, Brass Bands and Nickel Pianos),* compiled and annotated by Samuel Charters. RBF 17.
   5. *Jazz: New Orleans.* Edited by Frederic Ramsey, Jr. Folkways Records. FJ 2803.
   6. *Jazz: Some Beginnings.* Compiled and annotated by Samuel Charters. RF Records 31.
   7. *The Immortal King Oliver.* Milestone. MLP 2006.

Section 2

Intermediate Improvisation

Chapters 8–13 consist of the *alteration, extension, addition, and substitution* of the materials in Section 1. The relationships between categories (chapter titles) introduced in Section 1 should be woven closely together, both at a conceptual level and at the performance level, as you move ahead into Section 2.

Altered Patterns

8

A melodic line (here denoting a given thirty-two-bar tune as well as an improvised five-note melodic motive) can be altered by changing the rhythmic or accent placement of the original notes, or by adding or subtracting various pitches. The addition of pitches to given melodic material is probably the most common form of improvisation. For example, added pitches used in ornaments such as the trill, turn, and mordent are not written out even in nonjazz music, but are reduced to the well known symbols: *tr* , ∾ , and ⌇⌇. The jazz musician, while not given specific symbols with which to alter the given melodic lines or to build a solo from improvised motives, can still rely on several general guidelines to enhance the given material, and at the same time present a personal statement or interpretation. These guidelines can be summarized as follows:

1. Rhythmic displacement
   (a) Metric displacement
   (b) Accent
   (c) Augmentation
   (d) Diminution
2. Ornamentation
   (a) Scale or chordal interpolation within given melodic interval
   (b) Filling in rests with appropriate scale or chord tones
3. Combination of 1 and 2
4. Omission of some melodic (given) pitches
5. Combination of 2 and 4

Rhythmic Displacement

While a background **riff** remains essentially the same both rhythmically and metrically, the rhythmic function of a motive often changes. This change can be observed within many composed jazz tunes as well as throughout an improvised solo. Contrast the given riff patterns in "Boogie Stop Shuffle" with the use of motives in "Lobsters on Toast" or in Monk's improvisation on "Bag's Groove." Rhythmic development can take place even without adding pitches or rearranging the pitch order. Such development occurs when the placement of the motive in the measure is changed, the accents are redistributed, or the individual pitches of the motive are augmented or diminished in value.

The three-note motive in figure 8.1 is placed one beat later in measure 2 than in measure 1, thus providing tension and a feeling of incompleteness. This **rhythmic displacement** creates a need for added notes in measure 3—to complete the pattern. Measure 3 restates the first two pitches of the motive with shorter note values (diminution), partially fulfilling the need for pattern growth, but the two beats of rest between the first two and the third pitch of the motive help stretch the phrase into the fourth measure (augmentation). This motive is independent of a chord progression.

Figure 8.1

Rhythmic units of longer duration may be slightly more complex. Figure 8.2 consists of the same three pitches succeeded by another measure of material, which are then rhythmically displaced in measures 3 and 4. Although the pitches remain basically the same, the rhythmic alterations in the third and fourth measures provide momentum toward the quarter-note rest in measure 4, the highest tension point of the phrase. Rhythmic displacement also requires altered accent placement. From the introduction to accent placement in previous chapters, it will be observed that pitches F and E♭ trade accent positions from measure 1 to measure 3. In the first measure, F is accented because of its length, its prominence as the highest pitch, and its relationship to the previous accent, thus setting up an accent pattern or motive. E♭ is accented in measure 3 in order to keep the flow of the phrase intact. It carries the accent in anticipation of the climactic beat one of the next measure, a rest.

Figure 8.2

It has been shown in figures 8.1 and 8.2 how rhythmic displacement can occur by shifting the whole segment of melody to another beat or by augmenting or diminishing the durations of the rhythmic groups. Certainly one of the best sources of rhythmic displacement is the standard jazz tune literature. Not only can it help you become more familiar with different composers' individual styles of writing, but analysis of it also helps develop a deeper awareness of rhythmic development requirements during an improvisation.

Exercise XV
Play the given melodic pattern and its alterations in all keys (by ascending half steps).

(a) Each pattern separately: include given pattern, alteration a, alteration b, alteration c, and alteration d.

(b) Combined into larger
   units: each two-measure
   segment contains an
   alteration of the original
   pattern, while segments
   are also combined to
   form larger units.

Assignment 1

This assignment recalls the process used by Monk in his "Bag's Groove" solo (*Smithsonian* 10:1) discussed in chapter 4 (see fig. 4.4). All class members play the first two measures of the example, then each student in turn improvises a rhythmic displacement of the same three pitches in the next two measures. Complete a cohesive phrase and watch accents! (The following solos are for illustration only.)

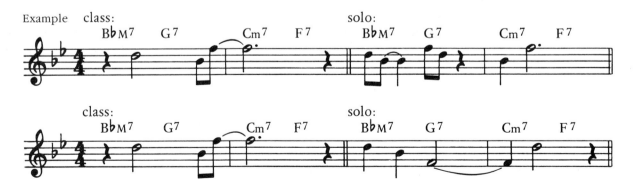

Assignment 2

Write a motive of your own to be played with the preceding chord progression. Teach it to the class by rote, then follow the same procedure as in Assignment 1. Can you transpose the motive–displacement progression to all keys?

Melodic Ornamentation

The given melodic line of a tune is a necessary indicator of the structural possibilities for improvisation. In addition to its rhythmic construction, the melody displays (1) the composer's specific ideas about the relationship between chords, (2) the composer's choice of important pitches for each chord, (3) how the chord tones move from one part of the progression to another, and (4) at what rate of speed these movements take place.

It is vitally important, therefore, that the given melody is carefully studied before any attempt at improvisation. After the melody and the chord progression are memorized, the next step is to add some of the chord tones to the melodic line. Note figure 8.3.

Figure 8.3

With the inclusion of only a few chord tones (original melody tones are circled), the line becomes more complex while still maintaining the basic melodic structure of the original tune. At the same time, however, rhythmic displacement (marked by Xs) adds interest to the line, while producing still another series of accent possibilities.

Only after the possibilities of ornamentation of the melody by added chord tones have been thoroughly examined is one able to understand the whole structure of the tune—how the rhythm, melody, and harmony relate to each other. After this has been accomplished (and it takes time), the performer might wish to fill in **nonchord** (scale) pitches between the chord tones to develop a smoother line. The relative number of nonchord tones to chord tones within a line is a matter of personal style and taste. So long as both are used toward a better definition of tension and relaxation in the phrase, they are acceptable. The original melodic pitches, therefore, help provide the basis on which the player can focus when employing ornamented scale/chord tones.

Figure 8.4 below combines scale pitches and chord tones between the original melody tones in a manner which further exemplifies rhythmic displacement but also reidentifies the basic melodic intervals.

Figure 8.4

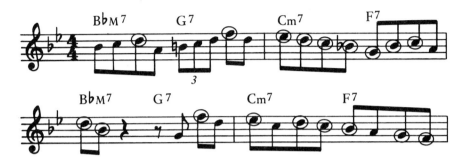

The first pitch of the original melody, D, is approached through two scale steps, B♭ and C, which displace its original metric position by one beat. The second original melodic pitch, B♭ (if the original durational space between the first two notes were left intact), would therefore by played against the B♮ of the G7 chord. Consequently, the original B♭ becomes a B♮ in the melody (the third degree of the G Mixolydian mode), narrowing the original melodic interval by a half step.

The insertion of scale pitches within a melodic line not only affects the rhythmic displacement or intervallic content of the original melody but can also provide it with new rhythmic possibilities. Beat 3 of measure 1, by combining three scale tones in succession, becomes an eighth note triplet in order to arrive at F by beat 4. While measure 2 consists of original melodic tones (except for the last pitch), measures 3–4 contain scale tones to help define the accent pattern of the phrase.

Another example of the combination of rhythmic displacement with added scale and chord tones is shown in figure 8.5. Here, the first five beats set up a melodic pattern based on the original line. The next five and a half beats, however, instead of following through the basic structure of the melody, continue to develop the first pattern on a different pitch level with a short extension. The last three pitches of the example finally refer to the original notes (with some omissions).

Figure 8.5

The process of developing new patterns from previously improvised material—and at the same time keeping the original structure in mind—is, of course, at a much deeper level of complexity, carrying ornamentation to its highest level. One must prepare for this by (1) careful memorization of the given melodic line and chord progression, by (2) the addition of chord tones into the rhythmically displaced melodic line, and by (3) combining scale and chord tones with the given melodic pitches.

Listen to "Blue 7" by Sonny Rollins (*Smithsonian* 10:3) and "Ko-Ko" by Charlie Parker (*Smithsonian* 7:7). Analyze the use of melodic patterns. For example, note the recurrence of the motives and their transformation throughout the compositions. Play some of your favorite patterns by ear, then listen to the recordings again.

Assignment 3

Motives

Rollins: "Blue-7"   Parker: "Ko-Ko"

BLUE 7 by Sonny Rollins

KO-KO by Charlie Parker. © 1946 Atlantic Music Corporation.
© 1974 renewed and assigned Atlantic Music Corporation.
Used by permission.

Ornament this melodic pattern over the blues progression, using the procedures described in Assignment 3.

Assignment 4

Omission of Melodic Pitches

As mentioned in the discussion of figure 8.5, some melodic pitches may be omitted to give room for the further ornamentation of a pattern. In fact, the number of pitches can be brought down to the structural pitches of a given melody with only one or two embellishing tones. See figure 8.6.

Figure 8.6

Further ornamentation practice can involve a combination of omitted and ornamented pitches in varying degrees of complexity. The importance of the original material must always be remembered, however, in any attempt to embellish or to improvise upon it.

Assignment 5

Ornament the melodies of some of the tunes listed in Assignment 1 (page 51) according to the guidelines presented in this chapter.

Assignment 6

From the accompanying cassette recording do Melodic Dictation C and Interval Dictation 3. Directions and required notation are in Appendix III.

Summary

A melodic line can be altered by (1) *rhythmic displacement,* which includes the displacement of meter and accent as well as the augmentation or diminution of the melody; (2) *ornamentation* of the melodic line by adding appropriate scale or chord tones either within a given melodic interval or during rests; (3) *combination* of (1) and (2); (4) the *omission* of some given melodic pitches; and (5) *combination* of (2) and (4).

Summary Activity

Play "Half Nelson" by Miles Davis from the following notation. Next, review the tune, "Lady Bird" (fig. 6.7), from which "Half Nelson" is derived, and discuss the means of melodic alteration in the latter.

HALF NELSON by Miles Davis. © 1948 (Renewed 1976) by Screen Gems–EMI Music, Inc. International Copyright Secured. All Rights
Reserved.

Tetrachord and Symmetrical Combinations

9

Most melodic patterns are based on scales built from tetrachords a perfect fifth apart and consist of only half-step or whole-step intervals. However, scales frequently employed in the jazz idiom contain

1. intervals of one and a half steps in addition to the traditional whole and half steps
2. tetrachords placed a tritone or even a minor sixth, rather than a perfect fifth, apart
3. tetrachords joined to pentachords, hexachords, or trichords
4. symmetrical formations unrelated or not divisible into tetrachords

The Harmonic Minor Scale

The first tetrachord of the harmonic minor scale consists of whole and half steps exclusively while the second tetrachord includes an interval of three half steps.

Figure 9.1

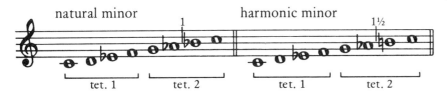

The one and a half step interval between A♭ and B♮ provides a unique color to the second tetrachord of the harmonic form of the scale. The B♮, which functions as a leading tone, also sharply increases the need for tension release via the tonic, a half step higher.

While these characteristics readily set this scale apart from the other minor forms (natural and melodic), it is especially important for the improviser, as for the composer, to explore these functions in the context of a musical composition.

Exercise XVI

(a) Play harmonic minor scales by ascending and descending minor seconds.

(b) Play the harmonic minor scale pattern around the Circle of Fourths.

Although it uses only pitches from the C harmonic minor scale, (a) of figure 9.2 contains information about neither the minor quality nor the harmonic form of the scale. Indeed, it may also be described as a major scale melody. It provides only the information that C is the tonic, G is the dominant, F is the subdominant, and B is the leading tone.

On the other hand, (b) exhibits the definitive characteristics of the harmonic minor quality in measure 1 (B to A♭). The minor quality (E♭) is assured in measure 2, and in measure 3 the harmonic minor qualities are confirmed.

Figure 9.2

Melody based on harmonic minor scale?

(a)

Melody based on harmonic minor scale

(b)   1.   2.   3.   4.

Since the harmonic form of the minor scale is defined within its second tetrachord, this assignment emphasizes that tetrachord.

Assignment 1

1. First, play the assignment as written.
2. You will note that as the melody ascends it keeps adding an extra high note and as it descends it keeps adding an extra low note. This continues throughout.
3. Play the assignment again, continuing beyond the last measure, and adding new high and low tones until you reach the limit of your instrument. Pianists should play the entire exercise, both hands together—watch fingering.
4. Play the assignment in all keys.

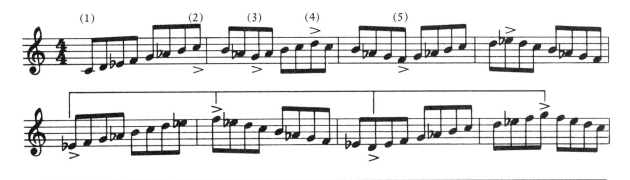

The Blues Scale

Both the first and second tetrachords of the blues scale contain an interval of *three* half steps. In addition, the first notes of each of the two tetrachords are a tritone apart.

Figure 9.3

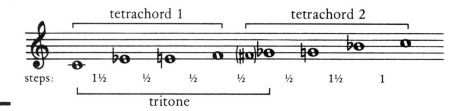

Exercise XVII

(a) Play blues scales by ascending and descending minor seconds.

(b) Play blues scale patterns (1234, 2345, 3456, etc.) around the Circle of Fourths.

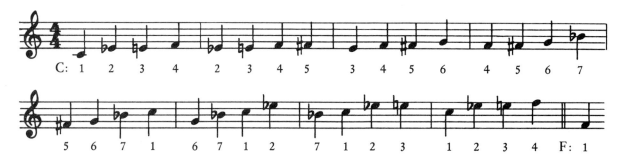

Since the blues scale is primarily a major scale with the addition of **blue notes** (flat 3,5,7) and the omission of the second and seventh scale steps, these alterations provide tension and coloristic possibilities. By alternating E♭ and E♮ with the tonic (C), for example, both major and minor qualities may be implied; and the fluctuation between F♯ and G, as well as between E♭ and E♮, can denote various degrees of tension related to both tonic and dominant functions. Ambiguity in relation to major and minor formations is also increased by the omission of the leading tone (B) which is replaced by the subtonic (B♭).

Although the blues scale includes two intervals containing three half steps (C to E♭ and G to B♭), its most striking characteristic is the addition of the flat third, fifth, and seventh. In actual practice (Coltrane's solo on "Blue Train" comes immediately to mind), soloists often incorporate blue notes as accessory pitches within other scale forms. Figure 9.4 could be interpreted either as evolving from the blues scale beginning on C with D as an auxiliary pitch, or from C Mixolydian with E♭ and F♯ as added pitches.

Figure 9.4

Blues scale or Mixolydian mode?

The necessary elements for the blues scale's particular flavor, consequently, are the *blue notes*. The minor third intervals that occur in both tetrachords simply provide the required pitches, while the performer has the option of filling in these thirds if desired.

Assignment 2

Play the line provided at various pitch levels using the ascending major scale (1), the descending major scale with added blue notes (2), and the blues scale, both ascending and descending (3).

The Pentatonic Scale

The pentatonic scale can be derived from the major scale: two pitches are deleted (and none added). Thus, what remains is five pitches containing no half steps whatsoever (fig. 9.5).

Figure 9.5

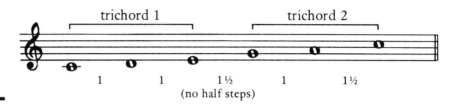

Exercise XVIII
Play the following pentatonic scale patterns, (a) and (b), and continue each by ascending and descending half steps.

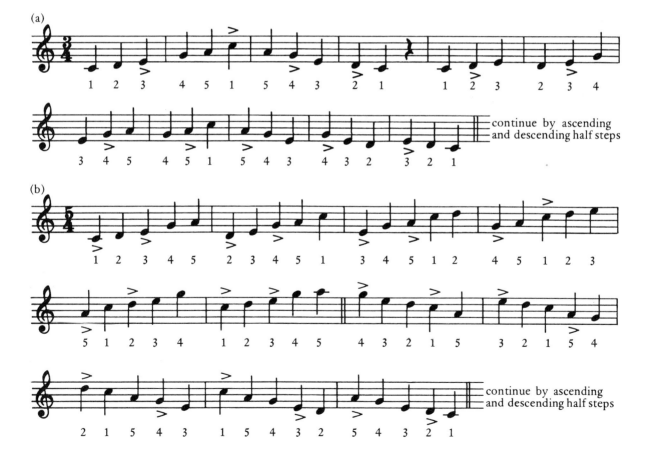

The absence of half-step intervals increases the degree of ambiguity (uncertainty) beyond that of the harmonic minor or blues scale.
Not only can the pentatonic suggest both major and minor forms but, in
addition, any of its five pitches can function as a tonic. See figure 9.6.

Figure 9.6

Use of pentatonic to suggest C major to A minor

Use of pentatonic to suggest A minor to C major

Consequently, the special properties of this scale are

1. its capacity to hint both major and minor qualities through
   implied tonics and dominants
2. its uncertain tonal center, which can be altered by continued
   stress on another scale pitch

This assignment emphasizes the ambiguities present in the pentatonic
scale. Play the scale ascending and then descending, adding new high
and low pitches to the limit of your instrument. Play the exercise on all
pitch levels.

Assignment 3

The Diminished Scale

Unlike the pentatonic or blues, the diminished scale is not derived from a major scale. Instead it is a symmetrical arrangement of half and whole steps, the alternate pitches of which spell out a diminished seventh chord.

One form of the scale consists of alternating half/whole steps and the other form alternates whole/half steps (fig. 9.7).

Figure 9.7

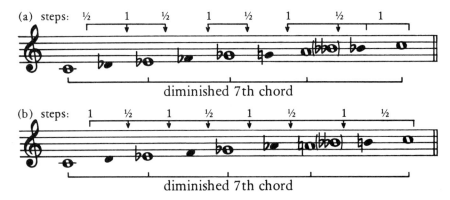

The choice of scale form is determined by musical content. While both scales in figure 9.7 outline the C diminished seventh chord, the intervening pitches outline a *different* diminished seventh chord: (a) contains a D♭ diminished seventh and (b) contains a D diminished seventh chord. Thus the particular scale selection will be based on *both* diminished seventh chords present within the scale.

Exercise XIX
Play the following diminished scale patterns (scale numbers not included).

(a) Whole/half steps (W/ H). Play around the Circle of Fourths.

(b) Half/whole steps (H/W). Play around the Circle of Fourths.

(c) Play as notated. Each pattern adds one pitch to either the W/H or the H/W form of the scale. Continue the pattern beginning on the remaining scale steps; then *descend,* using the same rhythm.

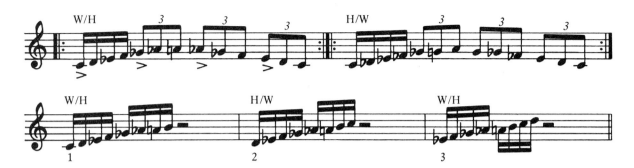

In addition, the player might combine segments of one scale form with the other (fig. 9.8), which outline a minor seventh chord in addition to the original diminished seventh.

Figure 9.8

combination of W/H with H/W $= \dfrac{\text{Gm}7}{\text{C}°7}$

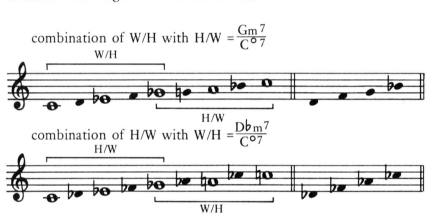

More advanced players might also use other combinations of intervening pitches to spell a dominant seventh chord (fig. 9.9).

Figure 9.9

combination of W/H/H/W with W/H $= \dfrac{\text{E}7}{\text{C}°7}$

Exercise XX
Play the following scale
combinations by ascending
half steps.

Play the following:

Assignment 4

  (a) The first five pitches W/H then H/W, repeat, then continue down
       by half steps

  (b) The W/H form of the scale: 1,2,3, etc., followed by 2,3,4,5, etc.,
       which becomes a H/W arrangement. Continue with 3,4,5,6, etc.

Since the diminished scale is derived from the diminished seventh chord, it is used much the same way melodically as the chord is used harmonically, i.e., to provide tension or a dominant function. Contrasting with the scales previously discussed in this chapter, the diminished scale is not often considered as having its own tonic, but as a dominant or dominant substitute for another tonic or tonal center.

Summary

In addition to scales built from tetrachords a perfect fifth apart and consisting of only half or whole steps, the jazz player often uses scales that contain

1. some intervals of one and a half steps
2. tetrachords placed a tritone (or larger) apart
3. tetrachords joined to nontetrachord formations, such as trichords, pentachords, or hexachords
4. symmetrical formations unrelated or not divisible into tetrachords (such as harmonic minor, blues, pentatonic, and diminished scales)

Summary Activity

Play "1321 at 8:50". This composition contains scale fragments which, by now, should be familiar to you. Analyze the scale segments used in the melodic line, then play the tune up to tempo and improvise on the changes. Use scales learned in this chapter as the basis for your solo.

* melodic pitches 1st time only

1321 AT 8:50 by Joan Wildman. © 1984 by Joan Wildman.

Chord Extension, Addition, and Substitution

10

Chord Extension

In the jazz tradition, triads are seldom found. Instead, seventh, ninth, eleventh, and thirteenth chords are the common practice. The isolated triad tends to create uncertainty. As an example, the C major triad (played alone and without context) could be the tonic (I) in C major, the subdominant (IV) in G major, and the dominant (V) in F major (see fig. 10.1).

Figure 10.1

CM: I   GM: IV   FM: V

On the other hand, without need for any further progression of chords, a diatonic dominant seventh chord accurately defines a key. The C7 does not relate diatonically to any key except F major (fig. 10.2). The only other diatonic major-minor seventh chord occurs as IV7 in melodic minor and is relatively rare.

Figure 10.2

FM: V7   or   Fm: V7   (only)

95

Hence, whereas a C major triad defines only a C major triad, a C7 chord, in addition, defines chord function (V7) and has the need for resolution to the tonic. Extended chords (seventh, ninth, eleventh, and thirteenth chords) include additional scale pitches and supply increased opportunities for tension and tonal color in harmonic progression.

The thirteenth chord includes all the pitches from its scale. In other words, as the V7 of C major (G7) is extended to its thirteenth (fig. 10.3), all the pitches of the chord are depicted horizontally by the Mixolydian mode. Likewise, a D minor thirteenth chord relates to D Dorian.

Figure 10.3

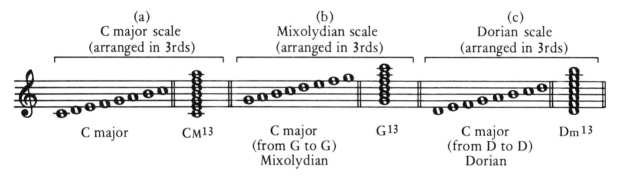

Qualities of dissonance, intensity, and stress differ greatly as seventh chords are extended into thirteenth chords. Each new third added above the triad thickens the chord and creates additional tension.

Exercise XXI
In (a) and (b), play the major scale and then the 13th chords built on ii, V, and I of the key. Continue around the Circle of Fourths.

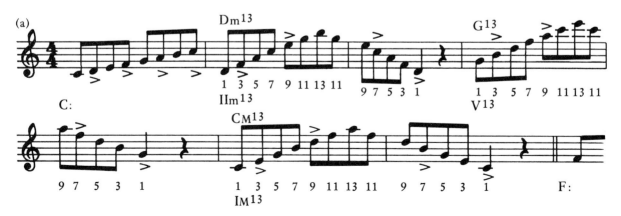

Play the following on your instrument, transposing an octave or two lower if necessary. The melodic pattern contains some tension of its own, but additions of the seventh, ninth, eleventh, and thirteenth factors demonstrate how tension can be increased by degrees.

Assignment 1

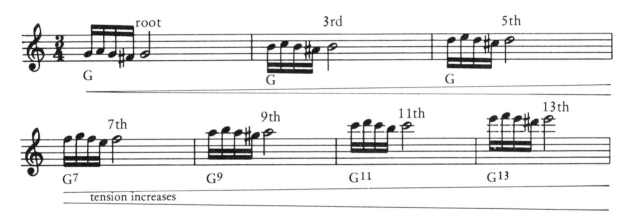

While the relative level of thickness and tension can be regulated within a single chord by adding thirds to the triad, the potential for variety is increased even further when chords are joined together in a harmonic progression. In short, an improviser can heighten the effect of a melody by increasing and decreasing harmonic tension at the proper moment throughout each phrase. The effect is somewhat like breathing—inhaling creates tension (takes more physical effort) and exhaling releases that tension.

Figure 10.4 (a) is the notation of the first ii–V–I melodic example from the accompanying cassette tape. The melody reaches its tension peak at X, which is the seventh of the V7 chord. While the ii–V–I progression itself provides an automatic thrust toward the V7 chord, the tension of V7 can be further increased by the use of the ninth (shown in (b). Note that the level of relaxation heard in the I chord in (b) is somewhat less than that of the tonic chord in (a)—the final two notes of the melody do not return to the tonic note C, but end on 5 (G) and 3 (E) of the chord.

Figure 10.4

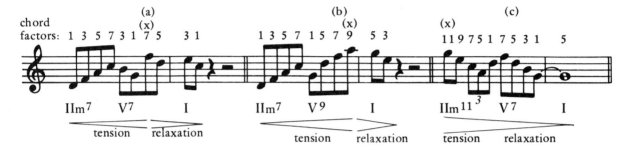

Consequently, although a ii–V–I progression by itself implies a tension shape (such as that seen in fig. 10.4), that shape can be modified or changed into another shape by the use of chord extensions.

Assignment 2

Write two melodic lines using the progression and tension shapes given. Use chord extensions when appropriate.

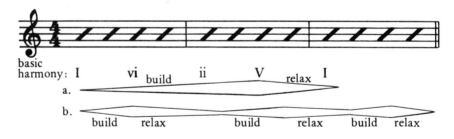

Added Chords

While the ii–V–I progression is most often employed to establish a tonal center, other chords are frequently added to this progression to intensify the journey toward the tonic. Of all diatonic chords added to ii–V–I, the vi chord predominates because it extends the series of ascending fourth progressions. If even further extension of the progression is desired, the iii chord, a perfect fourth below the vi, can also be included. The result is iii–vi–ii–V–I.

Diatonic triads

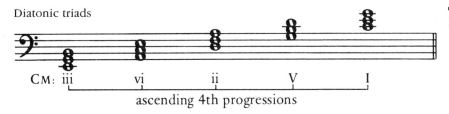

CM: iii   vi   ii   V   I

ascending 4th progressions

Figure 10.5

Often the ascending perfect fourth progressions (fig. 10.5) can be amplified by changing the quality of specific triads. In the progression, iii–vi–ii–V–I, the three successive minor chords can be changed to major to provide III–VI–II–V–I (fig. 10.6). Added sevenths to confer a dominant quality upon all chords except the final tonic provide optimum strength for this chord series as it proceeds toward the tonic.

Figure 10.6

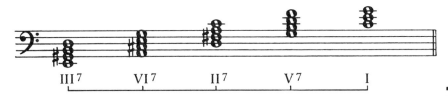

III⁷   VI⁷   II⁷   V⁷   I

Exercise XXII
Play the following III, VI, II, V progressions and continue around the Circle of Fourths.

Probably the most explicit examples of chord relationships that promote (and prolong) the tension level toward the tonic are the so-called "rhythm changes" in figure 10.7.

Figure 10.7

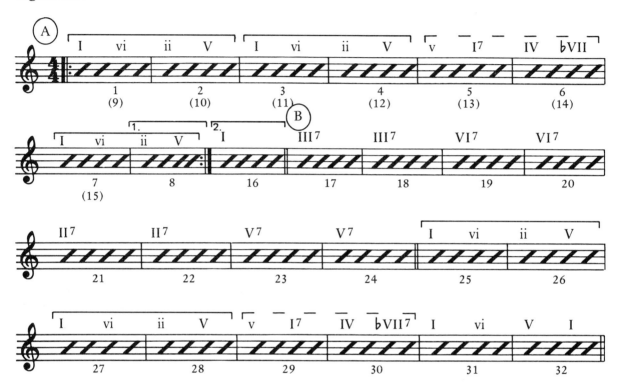

The basic progression in the A section is I–vi–ii–V–I. However, the I chord appears only at the beginning of each segment of the pattern I–vi–ii–V, while tension builds until the sixteenth measure, where the tonic goal is finally realized as the culmination of the progression.

Tension is maintained throughout the B section by chords of ascending fourths leading toward the dominant and by the transformation of these diatonic chords into dominant sevenths (III7–VI7–II7–V7). The reiteration of the eight-measure section A follows, ending on a I chord at the end of the composition.

Chords are often added in a progression to extend the motion toward the tonic. Neither the roots of the chords nor their modal quality necessarily reflect the tonic key, however. In the B section of the rhythm changes of figure 10.7, such chords function as unresolved dominant sevenths from measures 17–22 until the dominant of the original key finally appears in measures 23–24.

Additional clarification is needed for the sections marked with a dotted line, measures 5–6 and 29–30. These passages can be translated as a ii–V7–I in the key of IV, thus establishing a new temporary tonal center, which further lengthens the passage toward the original tonic.

Rather than confusing the tonality, this introduction of a new temporary key serves to emphasize the subdominant by elevating it to the status of a tonic. In further delaying the progression to the tonic of the original key, however, the bVII7 not only weakens the effect of the IV but also implies that the harmony will proceed another fourth higher (to bIII). Consequently, the example of figure 10.8 stresses the fact that, in addition to adding individual chords (such as iii and vi), progressions taken from other keys (like the subdominant) are also used to delay the ultimate resolution to the tonic chord. (Review transitory keys in chapter 5.)

Figure 10.8

| C major: | v | I⁷ | IV |
| F major: | ii | V⁷ | I |

C major: v   I^7 IV
F major: ii   V^7 I

Play "rhythm changes", figure 10.7, in all keys, beginning in Bb and continuing by ascending half steps.

Assignment 3

Listen to the harmonic progression in "Lester Leaps In" (*Smithsonian* 6:1). Notate the progression. Next, listen again to Don Byas' recording of "I Got Rhythm" (*Smithsonian* 7:5). How does the progression differ from "Lester Leaps In"?

Assignment 4

Play "Oleo." Incorporate added chords into your solo.

Assignment 5

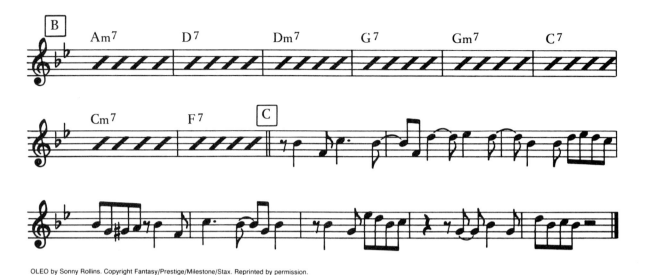

OLEO by Sonny Rollins. Copyright Fantasy/Prestige/Milestone/Stax. Reprinted by permission.

The added chords discussed thus far have been only the structural (most important) chords of the composition. Frequently, however, the improviser inserts additional chords or progressions between the given harmonies. These are usually diatonic chords in the original key or various ii–V–I combinations related to the specific given harmony. Figure 10.9 illustrates the use of chords and progressions added by improvisers in the twelve-bar blues.

Figure 10.9

Added chords and progressions in twelve-bar blues

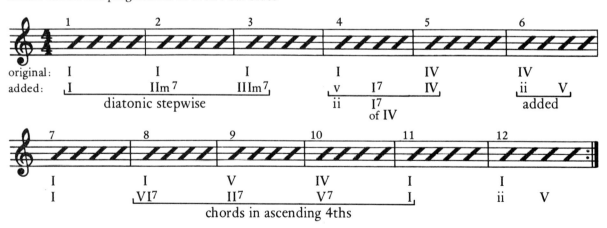

Measures 2 and 3 (fig. 10.9) continue a diatonic progression in the tonic key, thus prolonging the function of the I chord. In measure 4, the ii–V of the key of the subdominant points toward the structural significance of the IV chord in the next measure. The same procedure occurs with the I chord in measures 6–7. Measures 8–11 move in dominant sevenths toward the final tonic in ascending perfect fourth progressions. And, finally, the twelfth measure provides an added ii–V, or turnaround, toward the I chord in the next chorus.

Substitute Chords

In the midst of an ascending fourth progression of dominant seventh chords (fig. 10.9, measures 9–10), a II7 is substituted for a V (measure 9) and a V7 for a IV (measure 10). In this instance, the overall dominant seventh progression supersedes the tension of the given V–IV progression. Consequently, the added dominant seventh chord progression (measures 8–11) also doubles as a substitute chord progression (measures 9–10).

Substitute chords can be inserted by the performer, either in relationship to a larger progression as described, or on the level of each individual chord. The most common type is called the **tritone** (three whole steps) substitution (fig. 10.10). *Any dominant seventh chord can be substituted for another dominant seventh chord when the roots of the two chords are a tritone apart.*

Figure 10.10

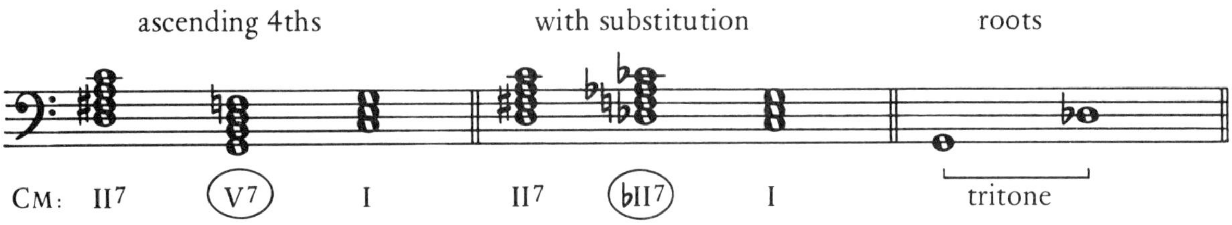

The tritone substitution is acceptable to the ear even though the roots of the two chords (original and substitute) bear an ambiguous relationship to each other. Nevertheless, smoothness is achieved in the substitute chord since the third and seventh of the two chords are interchangeable, i.e., the tritones of both chords have the same pitches (but not the same letter names). See figure 10.11.

Figure 10.11

original
chord   substitution   tritones extracted

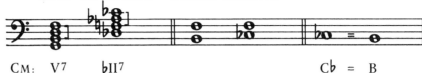

CM: V⁷   ♭II⁷   C♭ = B

Exercise XXIII
Play the following tritone substitutions.
(a) Play by ascending half steps.

(b) Play around the Circle of Fourths.

(c) Play by ascending half steps. G7 *or* D♭7 (1–5 of each chord, 3–5 of each chord, 5–7 of each chord).

D♭:

In a ii–V–I progression, the tritone substitution enables the roots to descend chromatically; ii–V–I becomes ii–♭II–I. Thus, the tritone substitution can become part of a substitute or added chord progression, depending on the musical context. The chord progression of the "Wildwoman Blues" (on cassette recording) contains numerous tritone substitutions (fig. 10.12).

Figure 10.12

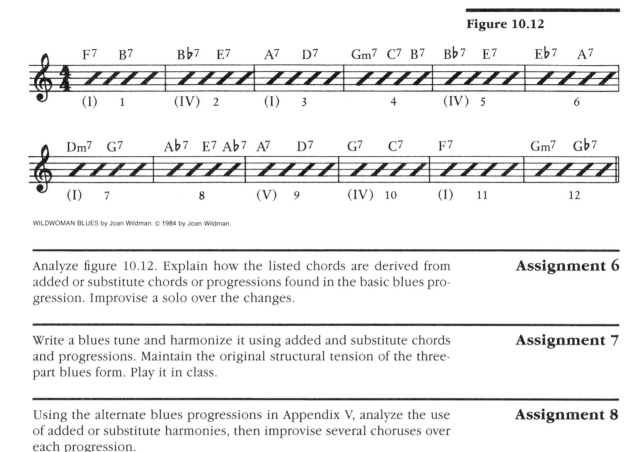

WILDWOMAN BLUES by Joan Wildman. © 1984 by Joan Wildman.

Analyze figure 10.12. Explain how the listed chords are derived from added or substitute chords or progressions found in the basic blues progression. Improvise a solo over the changes.	**Assignment 6**

Write a blues tune and harmonize it using added and substitute chords and progressions. Maintain the original structural tension of the three-part blues form. Play it in class.	**Assignment 7**

Using the alternate blues progressions in Appendix V, analyze the use of added or substitute harmonies, then improvise several choruses over each progression.	**Assignment 8**

Placement of Added and Substitute Chords

Added and substitute chords can be combined within a progression in many different ways, depending upon the structure to be embellished. The purpose of adding or substituting chords is to enhance an existing progression, not to destroy it. Therefore, the following three steps can be used as a guide and will be explained in detail below: (1) define the key centers, (2) determine the relative importance of tonic chords, and (3) assemble alternate chord structure.

Step 1. **Define the Key Centers** Temporary tonic chords are symbolized by a M7 chord in major keys and by a minor triad in minor keys. Finding the key center (even a temporary center), symbolized by this M7 or a minor triad, is important because it represents the release of tension (fig. 10.13). The chords prior to the tonic create stress, which is dissipated only when the I chord has finally been played.

Figure 10.13

Temporary tonics

Chords written out

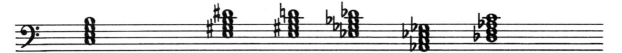

The original progression (fig. 10.13) contains three M7 chords: CM7, EM7, and DbM7. These tonics represent the points where tension is released and are thus to be considered further.

Step 2. Determine the Relative Importance of Tonic Chords The three tonic chords (CM7, EM7, and DbM7) are not of equal importance. A cursory glance at the melody shows that the B at the beginning of the melody is later transformed into its enharmonic equivalent, Cb. The G# (fourth note of the melody) undergoes the same change—from G# to Ab. Furthermore, the entire second phrase consists of the last two notes of the first, enharmonically spelled (see fig. 10.14).

Figure 10.14

B in CM7 and EM7 becomes: Cb   G# becomes Ab

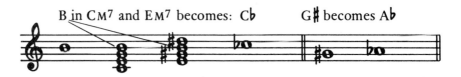

B is the first pitch and is a factor of the first two tonics. But when B becomes C♭ (in the second phrase), it approaches the D♭M7 (tonic) as a flat seventh, thus losing most of its stability. On the other hand, the G (second note) begins strongly as the fifth of the CM7 chord before losing its stability as it is changed to a G♯ in the fourth measure. As A♭ it rises in importance as the root of the A♭7 for four beats and takes on even more significance as the fifth of the final tonic D♭M7.

Tonic chords occurring at the end of a phrase have considerably more substance than those in the middle, and so the D♭M7 final chord achieves more prominence than the EM7 in measure 3. While the keys of C (first phrase) and D♭ (second phrase) have approximately the same duration, the first phrase, by virtue of its two different tonic chords, is weak and indeterminate. In contrast, the second phrase is strengthened by the ii–V–I progression in D♭ major.

Consequently, in order of importance, the three tonal centers rank as follows: *most important* is D♭ major, followed by C major, and finally E major.

Step 3. Assemble Alternate Chord Structure In figure 10.15, the diatonic chords prolong the key centers and a dominant, or a ii, chord forecasts the beginning of a new one.

Figure 10.15

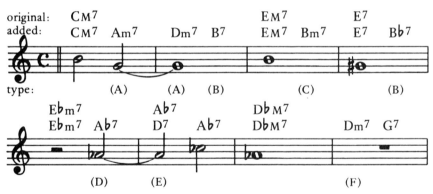

BEFORE FOUR by Joan Wildman. © 1984 by Joan Wildman.

(A)= Diatonic chords
(B)= Dominant of the next chord
(C)= ii of next chord
(D)= Dominant of preceding chord
(E)= Added tritone chord
(F)= Added ii-V

Whereas figure 10.15 employs only added chords, figure 10.16 combines chord extensions with added and substitute chords.

Figure 10.16

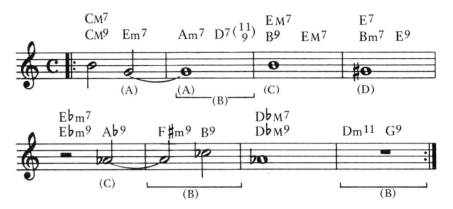

BEFORE FOUR by Joan Wildman. © 1984 by Joan Wildman.

(A) = Diatonic chords
(B) = Substitute ii-V
(C) = Added dominant
(D) = Added ii

Note that in figure 10.16 each measure contains an extension of the seventh chord. Figure 10.17 contains yet another series of added, substitute, and extended chords and progressions.

Figure 10.17

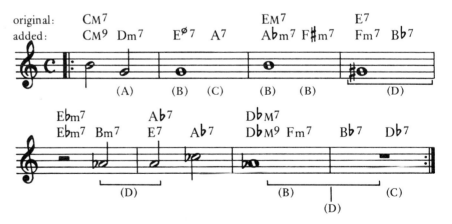

BEFORE FOUR by Joan Wildman. © 1984 by Joan Wildman.

(A) = Diatonic chords
(B) = Rootless chords
(C) = Tritone substitution
(D) = Substitute ii-V

In all three versions of "Before Four" (figs. 10.15, 10.16, 10.17), the basic structure of the given progression is maintained throughout. The M7 chords are preserved intact in figures 10.15 and 10.16 (although the EM7 is delayed for two beats in fig. 10.16). In figure 10.17 the EM7 chord is less definite owing to the use of rootless chords and a smoother movement to the D♭ tonic. Indeed, through the use of different chords or harmonic rhythm, a nearly infinite number of other possibilities exist for harmonizing the two phrases illustrated.

Analyze the progressions that follow and write alternate chords, maintaining the function of the original material.

Assignment 9

Other Dominant Substitutions: Two Common Tones

The dominant borrowed from another tonality is often used in place of the original. Perhaps the most common substitution occurs where the chords share two tones in common (see fig. 10.18).

Figure 10.18

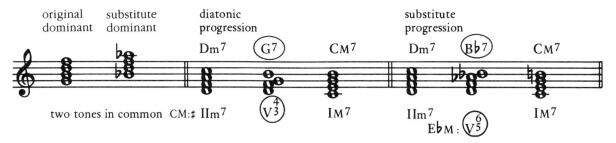

Whereas the two chords (original and substitute) in a tritone substitution contain a common tritone, this type shares a minor third (in fig. 10.18, D and F).

The increased tension created by the substitute dominant can be further enhanced by preceding it with a supertonic (ii) chord of the same key. In this instance, then, the original dominant chord is exchanged for a ii–V progression in another key (fig. 10.19).

Figure 10.19

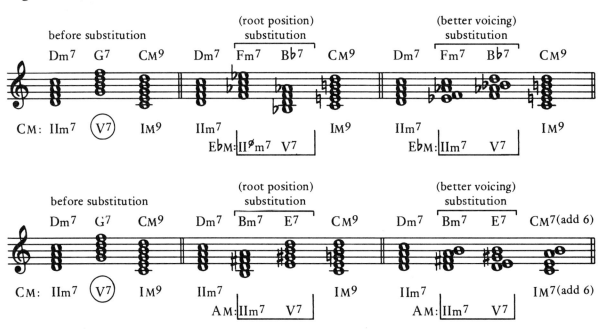

Note that root of both substitute chords lies a minor third from that of the original dominant.

One Common Tone

Also effective are substitute dominants from other keys that contain only one note in common with the original (fig. 10.20). These can also be preceded by their ii chords.

Figure 10.20

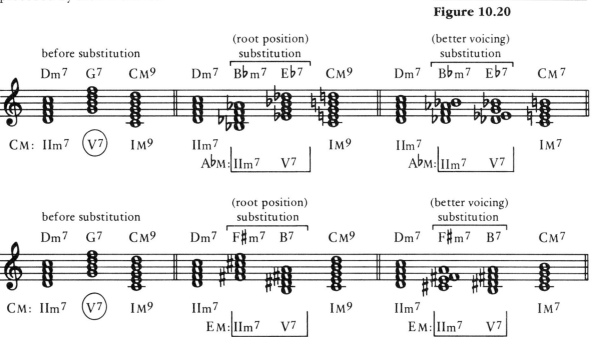

Note that the root of each substitute chord lies a major third from that of the original dominant.

No Common Tones

When the roots of the two chords (original and substitute) lie a major or minor second apart, no common tones are available. Although not found as frequently as those above, substitutions of this type are sometimes quite effective (fig. 10.21).

Figure 10.21

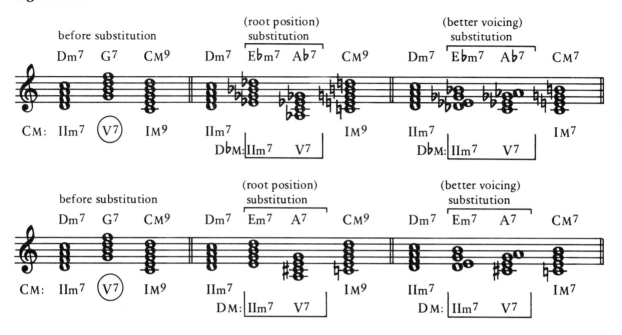

Deleted-Root Chords as Substitutes

As an imaginative diversion, the root of a chord can sometimes be omitted, producing a somewhat more delicate, if less definite, result (fig. 10.22). Most improvisers limit this device to the tonic chord, where it is most effective.

Figure 10.22

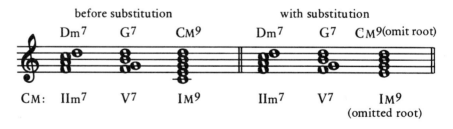

Assignment 10   Play ascending and descending m2s from the ii–V sequence of the accompanying cassette tape.

Summary

The extension, addition, or substitution of chords within a progression can be used to highlight the original structure. The process includes (1) the definition of key centers, (2) the determination of the relative importance of tonic chords, and (3) the assembly of the altered progression.

The choice of altered progressions often depends upon the common tone possibilities between the original dominant chord and its substitution. Although chords with two common tones are probably substituted most often, possibilities also exist between chords with one or even *no* tones in common.

Summary Activity

Play "You Stepped out of a Dream," which follows, then reharmonize the tune using extended, substitute chords, or added progressions. Write an arrangement for four horns.

The Addition or Substitution of Nondiatonic Scales and Chords within a Key

11

Relationships between Substitute Chords and Scales

Chords added to or substituted for basic progressions necessitate appropriate accompanying scale patterns for use in improvisation. As described in chapter 10, the first step in reharmonizing a tune is to observe the temporary tonal centers around which tension can be developed. In writing or improvising an arrangement, it is necessary to concentrate on the goal or target chord (usually IM7) in order to provide the appropriate suspense. The harmonic complexity that develops through the insertion of alternate harmonies presents problems in satisfying the needs of the substitute cadences and at the same time concentrating on the next tonal center.

Scales or scale patterns supply a unifying factor that can encompass both substitute or added chords and progressions. For example, in the ii–V–I, the ii implies Dorian, the V suggests Mixolydian, and the I indicates the major scale; yet, all three share the same seven tones. With relative ease, an improviser can plan ahead to the I chord while improvising through the ii and V, building melodic lines from the major scale that reflect the second (ii) and fifth (V) degrees. Similarly, in a series of ii–V progressions representing different tonal centers, it is important to utilize the same approach, concentrating on the scale accompanying each ii–V without the complications required in focusing on each separate Dorian and Mixolydian mode (see fig. 11.1).

Figure 11.1

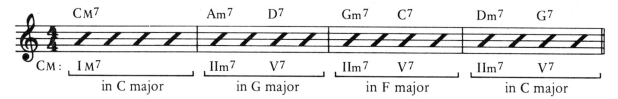

This process of simplification not only facilitates the journey through a temporary key center but is also invaluable in the memorization of tunes. The sixteen-bar tune, "Lady Bird" (*Smithsonian* 9:2), for example, implies the keys of C–E♭–C–A♭–G–C.

Assignment 1

Listen to "Django" (*Smithsonian* 10:4). Play with the recording and memorize the tune by relating one key relationship to another including shifts of mode (major to minor or vice versa).

If one keeps in mind the tonal centers implicit in substitute ii–V progressions, scale relationships themselves can also be substituted for additional color or a more ambiguous flavor. In regard to the tritone substitution (previously explained), it is possible that a scale substitution can be inserted during a dominant (V) function reflecting both the original and its tritone substitute (a diminished scale).

In the key of C major the half-step diminished scale built on the root of the V chord is

Diminished: G A♭ B♭ C♭ D♭ D E F G
Mixolydian: G A B C D E F G

The diminished scale contains all the pitches of the tritone substitute—in this instance D♭7. To add color to a dominant chord of long duration, the improvisation could alternate between the Mixolydian (for the diatonic dominant) and the diminished (for the tritone substitution), as in figure 11.2.

Figure 11.2

circled notes   - part of G half-step diminished scale
noncircled notes - part of G Mixolydian scale

For even more variety of color it is possible to use the dominant's diminished scale throughout a ii–V progression as shown in figure 11.3.

Figure 11.3

think CM: G half-step diminished scale
        Db half-step diminished scale

In figure 11.3, improvisers might find it easier to relate the diminished scale to the Db major scale, which begins a half step above the tonic C.

The same half-step diminished scale built on G contains, in addition to the pitches of the Db7 chord, the complete spelling of two other dominant seventh chords—E7 and Bb7—which are incidentally also a tritone apart. Needless to say, this scale can be used in any situation involving these chords. The whole-step diminished scale built on G, on the other hand, contains the pitches of two tritone groupings of dominant sevenths: C7–F♯7 and A7–Eb7. Note figure 11.4.

Figure 11.4

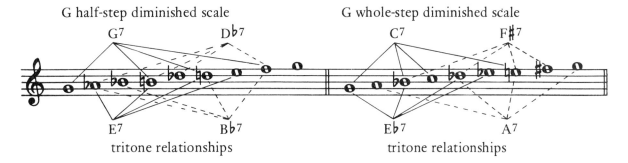

tritone relationships   tritone relationships

Exercise XXIV

Play the following ii-V patterns, (a) and (b), which contain diminished scale fragments. (Key relationship: descending major seconds)

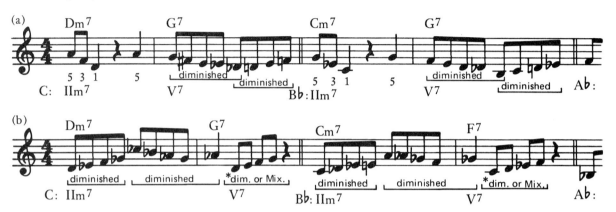

*This tetrachord can suggest either 5-6-7-1 of Mixolydian or W/H of a diminished scale.

Assignment 2

Write the G♯ and A diminished scales and diagram the dominant seventh chords formed both from the half- and whole-step forms. Then, play appropriate melodies based on diminished scales over the ii–V (major 2nd descending) and ii–V (major 2nd ascending) in Appendix IV.

The Relationship between the Blues Scale and I–IV–V

Not only can nondiatonic scales add color to a ii–V, but the blues scale can also be applied to all chords in a twelve-bar blues progression. Certainly the basic progression is a diatonic I–IV–V, and it follows, since the blues scale is derived from a major scale, that it is appropriate to use its derivatives in a blues harmonization. Especially effective in a variety of ways, the blues scale works equally well with tonic, dominant, or subdominant chords. It is precisely the unusual arrangement of the blues scale that permits the melody to work equally well with all three harmonies.

Melodic figure based on blues scale

Figure 11.5

Exercise XXV
Play the following patterns derived from the blues scale in all keys with the accompanying cassette recording of the twelve-bar blues.

(a) Continue playing the pattern with the cassette recording by ascending half steps.

(b) Continue with the pattern through the blues progression by ascending half steps.

(c) Continue with the pattern through the blues progression by ascending half steps.

Assignment 3

With the cassette recording (Appendix V) improvise blues melodies in all keys as you experiment with the blues scale.

The Relationship between the Pentatonic Scale and Diatonic Chords

Not only does the *addition* of blue notes to the major scale add ambiguity, but also the *omission* of the second, sixth, and seventh scale degrees creates further uncertainty. In a similar manner, the pentatonic scale can be employed with single chords or throughout long passages to furnish ambiguity. As described in chapter 9, individual pitches can be emphasized to accentuate major or minor colors. With the seventh scale degree missing, the pentatonic implies dominant or tonic harmony equally. Note figure 11.6.

Figure 11.6

Obviously, the pentatonic scale is one of the "safest" scales for the aspiring improviser, but it has its drawbacks as well. As the tension-relaxation level remains relatively constant in this scale (because of the lack of half-steps), the performer must rely more heavily on the duration of pitches, their rhythmic vitality, and dynamic contrasts to ensure an interesting and musical result. While the pentatonic scale can be helpful in developing some concepts, inexperienced improvisers should soon learn to combine the tension-relaxation qualities of pitch with those of other musical elements. Scales endowed with half steps (the most common pentatonic scales have none) supply better opportunities for such tension than does the pentatonic.

The Relationship between Scale and Key

To summarize, the relationships between the scale and the key (assuming scale and key are not always the same) depend heavily on the intensity desired. Agreement between scale and key produces low tension, and clashes between the two bring about increased stress.

Fresh and exciting improvisation can be generated through exploitation of melodies based on scales that conflict with the key; through melodies outlining diatonic chords (ii–V) in other keys; through melodies based on substitute scales that suggest two harmonies simultaneously (such as G7 and Db7); and through scales, such as the pentatonic, that provide uncertainty and ambiguity. The prospects for success are increased when several of the above scale/key relationships are combined into the same solo.

Make up your own melodies for the ii–V progressions found on the accompanying cassette recording. Use any of the root movements outlined in Appendix IV. Use scale patterns that exemplify the progression.

Assignment 4

From the accompanying cassette recording, do Melodic Dictation D and Interval Dictation 4. Directions and required notation are in Appendix III.

Assignment 5

Choose a solo played on your own instrument from the *Smithsonian Collection.* Transcribe and play it with the record in class. Give examples of scales that add tension to the prevailing harmonies.

Assignment 6

Summary

The use of added or substitute ii–V progressions requires a focus upon the temporary target chord or key. Diminished, blues, or pentatonic scales can also be substituted for the diatonic scales of any temporary key.

Summary Activity

Refer to your reharmonization of "You Stepped Out of a Dream" (chapter 10). Memorize your progression and improvise upon the chord changes, applying segments of the scales discussed in the Summary to add to, or enhance, the desired color or to lend ambiguity to your solo line.

Analysis of "Confirmation" by Charlie Parker

12

The recognition of temporary key centers is essential to the preparation of substitute or added harmonies and is important also as an aid in memorization. Just as the structure of two melodies, built from the same scale, vary according to the stress placed on different pitches, **temporary tonics** also influence the shape of a composition through their relationships with the original tonal center. One tune in the key of F, for example, might contain several progressions centered upon D minor (a temporary tonic), while another focuses on C or G minor. The choice of specific temporary tonics (along with their duration), therefore, is the basic means by which the structure of each individual tune can be defined.

"Confirmation" by Charlie Parker

The first phrase of "Confirmation," rhythmically analyzed in chapter 7, begins in F major and is followed by a temporary modulation to D minor. The Cm7 to F7 progression in measure 5 then anticipates a further shift to Bb. Measures 6 through 8 provide rising levels of tension with ascending fourth progressions touching G major on the return to F major (measure 9). This section, illustrated in figure 12.1, consists of a diatonic movement of tonics.

Keys:	F	d	Bb	G	F
Temporary tonics:	I	vi	IV	II	I

Figure 12.1

The next eight measures (9–16) follow the outlines of the first eight except that the direction of measures 6–8 approaches the dominant, while measures 13–16 work toward the tonic (F). The change of direction begins in a subtle manner. The first chord of measure 6 is Am7, interpreted by the listener as a substitute I (Am7=rootless FM9), but it suddenly changes function and anticipates a ii when followed by D7. On the other hand, the FM chord of measure 14 firmly establishes the F major tonal center, with D7 simply acting as an altered vi7 (changed to M–m):

Measure 6:   Am7   D7
Measure 14:   F   D7

While measure 7 continues the ascending fourth movement with another dominant seventh (G7), eroding the expected G tonal center, the tension of the dominant of F major is finally resolved in measure 9. Conversely, measures 15–16 reiterate the tonal center of F, approaching the tonic through its ii–V progression.

Measures   7–9: G7   Gm7   C7(♭9)   F
Measures   15–16: Gm7   C7   F

The bridge section of the composition, measures 17–24, provides structural contrast by moving to a temporary tonic built on the subdominant—measures 17–20 are temporarily in B♭ major. The contrast is further heightened by the long duration of the B♭ tonal center. Moreover, in measure 21, the tension level rises dramatically with the E♭ minor triad pulling toward a D♭ tonal center. This arrival at D♭, although far removed from the parent key (F), is a substitute dominant leading to the dominant (C7) of F major. (Note that the D♭ chord is the tritone substitution for a G chord.)

Measures 23–24: D♭ Gm7 C7

When the "real" dominant (C7) occurs at measure 24, the tension subsides and there is a smooth transition to the ultimate relaxation—the F major tonic. The reappearance of the I chord in measure 25 also reintroduces the same basic melodic material found in the first sixteen measures. The harmonic scheme in measures 25–32 follows the same pattern as that of measures 9–16. This recurrence of the earlier material signals the last section of the tune. The formal structure of the entire thirty-two measures fits into the AABA scheme typical of many standard jazz tunes.

Measures: 1–8   9–16   17–24   25–32
   Form: A   A   B   A

While the overall form of "Confirmation" is not unusual, the specific tonal design is. In their own special way, the temporary tonal centers occurring in this composition endow the chord structure with its own special flavor. A similar interdependence of tonal centers and chord structure characterizes every other composition.

Assignment 1	Memorize "Confirmation." Pay close attention to the rhythmic organization of the tune in addition to its harmonic and melodic structure. Improvise on the tune. First, work through one section at a time, concentrating on the various temporary key centers. Then, improvise as many choruses as you can while maintaining the structure of the tune itself as well as the unity of your own solo. (Choose a tempo you can handle.)
Assignment 2	Analyze and compare the structures of two tunes such as: "Oleo" vs. "Confirmation"; "Autumn Leaves" vs. "Summertime"; or "I'll Remember April" vs. "How High the Moon" ("Ornithology"). Write down the temporary tonics and indicate their duration, then make a chart of each tune showing the temporary tonic scheme for the entire tune. *Memorize* the tunes you analyze.
Assignment 3	Write a thirty-two-bar composition using your own chord progression (include temporary keys).
Assignment 4	Play "Drop the Needle" on one of the sides of the *Smithsonian Collection*. Be able to analyze aurally the form of any of the tunes you hear (ABA, AABA, etc.). Can you hear the progressions? Try to play the roots of the chords as you listen to the recording.

Summary

A tune is dependent upon its temporary keys to emphasize or enhance its shape or structure. "Confirmation," for example, contains five "keys" within the first eight measures. Both contrast and increased tension occur during the bridge section (measures 17 to 24) through the shift to the temporary Bb tonic and the pull toward the key of Db in measure 21. The A section returns at measure 25 to produce a thirty-two-bar AABA form.

Summary Activity

From Assignment 3, play and improvise upon tunes written by other class members. Observe, as quickly as possible, the relationships between temporary key centers, and use that information to help organize your solo line.

Beat Placement

13

Just as a player is expected to transform scales and chords into personal musical statements, so it is with rhythm and articulation. After one relates to time as large-beat units and can propel energy toward the next goal through a coherent rhythmic phrase structure, one must be aware of the flexibility inherent within the time structure.

Playing Ahead and Behind the Beat

A beat can be either wide or narrow. For example, although each beat occurs as a "point" in time, try to envision the difference between the "point" made by an ultrafine-line pen and a magic marker. The ultrafine-line pen demonstrates the center of a beat, while the magic marker widens the possibilities, allowing a loose, swinging, personal approach to time on many different structural levels. A wide-beat conception is not just a haphazard reaction, however; it is idiomatic to the jazz style. Thus, one basic difference between ragtime and early jazz pianists is the relationship between left- and right-hand beat placement: ragtime pianists played both hands at the same time, whereas early jazz players played the left-hand notes slightly ahead of the right hand.

Listen to Scott Joplin's recording of "Maple Leaf Rag" (*Smithsonian* 1:1) and compare it with James P. Johnson's recording of "Carolina Shout" (*Smithsonian* 2:4).

Assignment 1

The difference between beat placement of the pianist's left and right hands has also been reflected in the functions of instrumental combinations. Traditionally, the rhythm section (pianist's left hand) plays further ahead of the beat than does the soloist (pianist's right hand).

Assignment 2

Listen to the wide-beat placement between the rhythm section and Sonny Rollins's playing in his recording of "Blue 7" (*Smithsonian* 10:3).

Within each rhythm section as well, a different kind of swing will result depending upon the relationship of the drummer's beat to that of the bass player. Some bass players prefer to stay in the middle of the beat and let the drummer go ahead, while others do just the opposite. (The pianist can reconcile both positions by staying in the middle or by fluctuating between players, depending upon phrase structure. The important thing is to recognize the difference—and do what is required.)

Exercise XXVI

(a) Listen to "Lunceford Special" by Jimmie Lunceford (*Smithsonian* 5:13).

(b) In the following notation (at measure 17 in the recording), play the two lines of (A) as a rhythm section: piano and guitar play the treble clef melody; bass plays the bass line; drums play in the middle of the beat. Note the *effect* of the treble playing ahead of the beat (because of the notation).

(c) Repeat the lines until the beat placement feels comfortable. Play with the record.

This assignment is specifically written for bass and drums although it should also be played by pianists (both lines), or by two horn players together.

Assignment 3

1. **X** = Choose any pitch.
2. An arrow above the note means:
    (a) ↑ = on the beat
    (b) ← = ahead of the beat
    (c) → = behind the beat

While varied beat placement between the soloist and rhythm section, or between rhythm section players themselves, might not be so readily apparent to the casual listener, changes in time relationships *within* a beat have been identified with stylistic changes throughout jazz history. The gradual evolution of the soloist's treatment of the eighth-note pattern, from the dotted-eighth and sixteenth of ragtime to the straight eighth notes of today's jazz fusion styles, demonstrates many periods of stylistic development. Along with the durational changes, and equally important, has been an accent shift from the first eighth note to the second.

Assignment 4

Play the following examples. Experiment by playing *on, ahead,* and *behind* the beat.

Suggested method:

1. First, all players *on* the beat.
2. Then, bass, drums *on* the beat with soloist *behind.*
3. Then, bass *ahead,* drums *on,* and soloist *behind.*
4. Drums and soloist vary relationships with pattern.

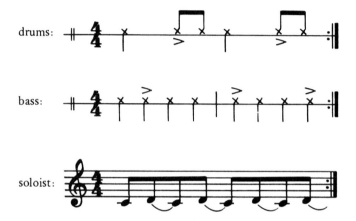

Asymmetrical Divisions

Increasing the possibilities of temporal relationships at the beat level (and extended beat level) is the use of **asymmetrical** division. This idea can range from the use of asymmetrical meters to the "sheets of sound" concept of John Coltrane in which the number of notes within a certain time frame is not so important as the overall cumulative sound. Although irregular divisions are most often associated with an instrumental soloist, the polyrhythms of a drummer (Elvin Jones, for example) can amply illustrate the use of irregular divisions of the beat as an accompanying device.

    While most standard jazz compositions are written in 4/4, metric groupings of three are also familiar: as a jazz waltz in 3/4 or perhaps as often, the blues played in 12/8. The metric combination of twos and threes is traditionally less common, although you will readily remember "Take Five" by Dave Brubeck with its three-plus-two

(♩♫♩ ♩♩) formation in 5/4. Many recent compositions, however, do contain meters of 5/4, 7/8, etc., or else contain a measure or two of an irregular meter within a 4/4 framework.

Play the following (a), (b), and (c) as fast as possible, several times in succession. Provide accents.

(a)

(b)

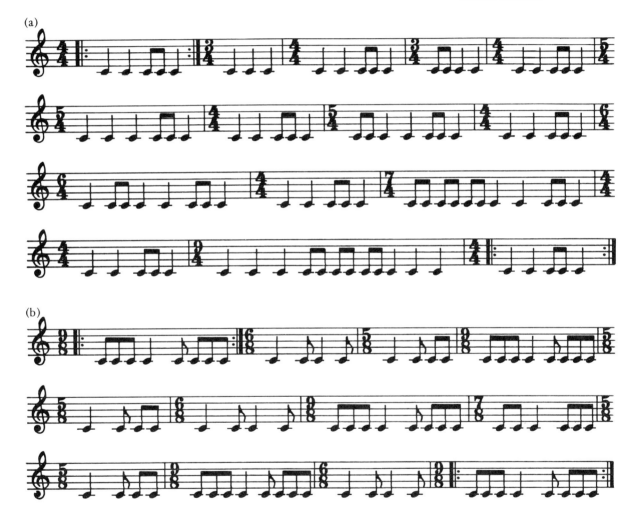

(c)

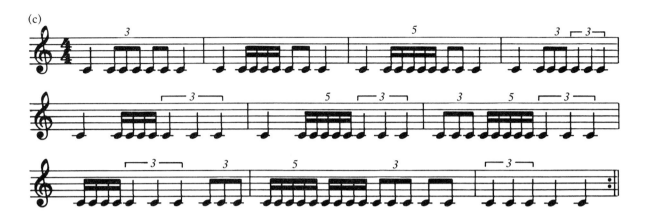

There are no further written exercises. By the time you are ready to work with the materials in section 3, you must focus directly on your own technical needs and construct materials to develop your personal style.

Assignment 5

Play Exercise XXVII (pp. 131–32). Using pitches from a pentatonic scale, change the pitch on each note. Play as fast as possible several times in succession.

Assignment 6

Listen to Sidney Bechet's recording (*Smithsonian* 2:3), and analyze the rhythmic structures from the point of view of (a) the soloist; (b) the rhythm section; and (c) the background players. Discuss beat placement on a larger level and also temporal relationships within the beat. Transcribe some of the riffs, and play them in the same style along with your own rhythm section.

Assignment 7

From the *Smithsonian Collection* (8:7), listen to Sarah Vaughan's recording of "Ain't No Use." Notice her placement of the beat in contrast to that of the rhythm section. Also, analyze the use of *triplets* vs. *duplets* throughout the recording.

Summary

A personal rhythmic sense must become incorporated into one's overall style of playing. One of the most distinctive elements of any player's style is the placement of the beat—ahead, behind, or in the middle of the pulse.

The divisions of both meter and individual beats can be irregular. Thus, meters as well as beats can be composed of various combinations of twos and threes.

Summary Activity

Choose any two cuts from two different recordings and try to isolate the beat placement of the individual players. Tap the pulse of (a) the bass player, (b) the drummer, (c) the pianist's left hand, and (d) the soloist. Try to listen to the beat placement of another player at the same time. Compare the beat placement between the players on one record with the other.

Section 2 Summary

Chapters 8–13 are an intermediate level presentation of the same basic concepts as outlined in chapters 1–7.

Chapter 8. Altered Patterns   Melodic lines are altered by rhythmic displacement, ornamentation, pitch omission, or any combination of these.

Chapter 9. Tetrachord and Symmetrical Combinations   The harmonic minor, blues, pentatonic, and diminished scales are formed from tetrachords, which include (a) intervals larger than a whole step or tones placed a tritone apart, (b) tetrachords joined to other formations larger or smaller, and (c) symmetrical groupings unrelated to or not divisible into tetrachords.

Chapter 10. Chord Extension, Addition, and Substitution   Chords can be extended, added to or substituted for the given progression. The key centers must first be defined and arranged according to their relative importance, before the alternate progression can be assembled. Although alternate progressions can be built around substitute dominants with one or no common tones, a chord containing two common tones probably is substituted most frequently.

Chapter 11. The Addition or Substitution of Nondiatonic Scales within a Key   The focus upon the target chord or temporary tonic must be retained throughout the process of adding or substituting ii–V progressions. Nondiatonic scales, such as the diminished, blues, or pentatonic, may be substituted for their diatonic counterparts.

Chapter 12. Analysis of "Confirmation" by Charlie Parker   The basic structure of a tune is animated through the use of transitory or temporary keys. "Confirmation," for example, a thirty-two-bar AABA tune, contains five "keys" in the first eight measures.

Chapter 13. Beat Placement   The beat can be placed ahead, behind, or in the middle of the pulse. Individual beat placement becomes a distinctive element of personal style.

Divisions of the beat, or meter, can be irregular. Thus, irregular groupings of two and three can be established within one beat, or as a meter signature (5/4, 7/8, etc.).

Summary Activity

Play the following composition as an ensemble piece for the whole class. (Pitches used in composition: B–C–C♯–D; E–F–F♯–G.)

1. Each student must be able to read (transpose) *each* line, providing suitable articulation and accents. (Make it swing!)
2. Decide the overall shape of the performance with regard to tension. (Perhaps you will start very softly, with only a few players, gradually build to a climax, and fade out as you started.)
3. Each performer can choose the lines he or she wishes to play and can play a different line when desired (depending upon the texture of the group as a whole).
4. After the ensemble has been rehearsed, a soloist should improvise, using appropriate scale combinations, over the ensemble texture. (Ensemble players must use a thinner texture while backing a soloist.)
5. Perform the composition from beginning to end, using your own musical instincts to guide the tension and relaxation.
6. Repeat each line as many times as desired.

SOMETIME by Joan Wildman. © 1984 Joan Wildman.

Additional Materials

Examples of some recent tunes *not* written in 4/4.

1. **3/4 meter:**
    "502 Blues" by Wayne Shorter
    "Domino Biscuit" by Steve Swallow
    "Gemini" by Jimmy Heath
    "Hullo Bolinas" by Steve Swallow
    "May Dance" by Dave Holland
    "Miyako" by Wayne Shorter
    "Saga of Harrison Crabfeathers"
    "Sweeping Up" by Steve Swallow
    "Trance" by Steve Kuhn
    "Unity Road" by Pat Metheny
    "Wild Flower" by Wayne Shorter
2. **5/4 meter:**
    "Conference of the Birds" by Dave Holland
    "Mevlevia" by Mick Goodrick
    "Watercolors" by Pat Metheny

3. **6/4 meter:**
   "Colors of Chloe" by Eberhard Weber
   "Empathy" by Richard Niles
   "Vashkar" by Carla Bley
4. **6/8 meter:**
   "12–4 2–4/Duplicates" by Jack Stock
   "Space Circus" by Chick Corea
   "Children's Song" by Chick Corea
5. **Other:**
   "Ad Infinitum" by Carla Bley (9/8 meter)
   "Wrong Key Donkey" by Carla Bley (7/4 + 5/4)

Discography

A. **Two recorded versions of the same composition**
   1. "So What"
      (a) Miles Davis (*Smithsonian Collection*)
      (b) Miles Davis (*Four and More*, Columbia, PC 9253)
   2. "Ko-Ko" (Cherokee)
      (a) Charlie Parker (*Smithsonian Collection*)
      (b) Clifford Brown (*Brownie Eyes*, Applause Records, APBL–2314)
   3. "Alabama"
      (a) John Coltrane (*Smithsonian Collection*)
      (b) John Coltrane (*Live at Birdland*, MCA Records A–49)
   4. "Off Minor"
      Thelonious Monk and John Coltrane (*Monk/Trane*, Milestone M–47011)
   5. [Nearly All Selections]
      Charlie Parker (*Bird/The Savoy Recordings, Mastertakes*, Savoy 5JL2201)
   6. "Naima"
      (a) John Coltrane (*Giant Steps*, Atlantic 1311)
      (b) John Coltrane (*Coltranology, Volume One*, Affinity Records AFF–14)
B. **Big bands of the thirties and forties**
   1. *The Big Band Sound.* RCA CCL2–0619(e) (includes Artie Shaw, Charlie Barnet, Count Basie, Les Brown, Blue Barron, Duke Ellington, among others)
   2. *Bunny Berigan and His Orchestra, 1936–38* (Almanac Records QSR 2414)
   3. *Billy Eckstine Orchestra, 1945* (Almanac Records QSR 2415)
   4. *Duke Ellington and His Famous Orchestra, 1941* (Almanac Records QSR 2439)
   5. *Chick Webb and His Orchestra, 1936* (Almanac Records QSR 2437)

Section 3

Advanced Improvisation

Whereas Section 1 describes the basic
concepts and activities involved in
improvisation, and Section 2 expands
the possibilities within this framework,
Section 3 discusses their *stylistic
application*.

Stylistic Alterations

14

When based on a preexisting or original melody, an improvised melodic line can provide variation through rhythmic displacement, ornamentation, omission, or complete lack of direct reference to the original (as discussed in chapter 8). This is not to say that the improviser ignores the given material, but instead fashions a logical contrast to it while creating a new and different melodic structure.

The idea of presenting a personal statement about given material, of course, is as old as the blues. Almost every performer throughout the history of jazz has had the opportunity to demonstrate originality, but only a few, more creative artists have managed to make such definitive statements as to create an entirely new and distinctive style. Among these innovative giants are Louis Armstrong, Charlie Parker, Miles Davis, and John Coltrane, who have permanently etched their individuality on the basic framework of tradition. Terms such *bebop, hard-bop,* and *modal playing* originated as individual concepts, but were soon adopted by a collective body of jazz performers and became stylistic references, indispensable to understanding melodic structure and style in jazz.

A detailed examination of neither individual playing styles nor of their historical significance is possible within these pages, but it is taken for granted by the authors that the reader is pursuing such background material concurrently with the study of this text.

While there is a tendency to group jazz artists into specific style periods when discussing their individual characteristics, the following discussion will focus on melodic lines (with examples from individuals) that may or may not fit into particular style categories. The distinctions among melodic types will be improvised melodies derived from

1. the harmonic structure
2. the scale structure
3. the motivic or intervallic structure

In all instances, instead of standard variation techniques (rhythmic displacement, ornamentation, etc.), the improviser creates new melodic relationships.

Melodies Derived from Harmonic Structure

Examples of melodies derived from harmonic structure can be found in jazz from Benny Goodman to Coleman Hawkins (or outside of jazz in the baroque continuo player). "Running the changes," however, becomes more complex with the insertion of added or substitute harmonies.

The presence of nonharmonic (nonchord) tones usually elevates the level of tension within a phrase. In addition to the concepts outlined in chapter 8, melodic phrase structure can actually be derived from the use of nonchord tones and their resolutions. In contrast to added dominant or ii–V melodic progressions that literally translate a vertical sonority into a linear one, individual pitches (as well as groups of pitches) can also be borrowed from contrasting harmonies, which not only increase the tension level but also mark the points of vertical stress that delineate each portion of the phrase.

Figure 14.1, from a phrase by Charlie Parker, shows nonchord tones and their resolutions along with the resultant tension vs. relaxation and structural relationships.

Figure 14.1

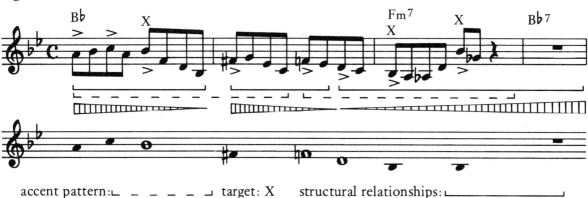

accent pattern:⌐ _ _ _ _ ⌐   target: X   structural relationships: ⌐_____⌐

KO-KO by Charlie Parker. © 1946 Atlantic Music Corporation. 1974 renewed and assigned © Atlantic Music Corporation. Used by permission.

The Xs depict the intermediate and final goals (target pitches) as the tension level rises throughout the phrase. The first B♭ is the root of the corresponding harmony, while the second and third B♭'s are nonchord tones. The accents provided by the soloist (indicated below the line in fig. 14.1) comprise the following rhythm:

The occurrences of nonchord tones and their resolutions correspond to the accent structure as shown on the lower staff: the nonchord tones A and C in the first measure prepare for the first target pitch B♭, which is their resolution note. The next nonchord tone, the F♯ of measure 2, followed by what appears to be an added C minor chord, finally descends to its resolution note F♮ on beat 3. Thus the tension level within the first measure and a half looks quite predictable: tension and release; tension and release; that is, until it becomes apparent that the F (measure 2) besides being a resolution note (for the F♯) is also the beginning of the next accent pattern. In addition, the accent pattern, as it occurred in measure 1, consisted of two nonchord tones followed by their resolution pitch. But the opposite is true in measures 3–4. The B♭ target pitch (measure 3, beat 1) becomes an accented nonchord tone, and the final B♭, also a nonchord tone, creates the highest level of tension in the phrase. Thus, the nonchord tones and their resolution and, in this instance, chord tones moving to nonchord tones, are the basic means by which the phrase structure has been made coherent.

Assignment 1

1. Listen to Coleman Hawkins's solo on "Body and Soul" (*Smithsonian* 4:4). Compare the harmonic treatment of his melodic lines with those of the Charlie Parker solo excerpt from "Ko-Ko."
2. Play Section A of "Body and Soul," which follows, until it is memorized.
3. Transcribe the first sixteen bars of Coleman Hawkins's solo on the composition.

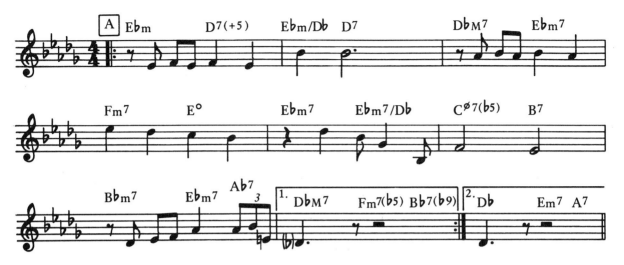

Melodies Derived from Scale Structure

While the excerpt from Charlie Parker's solo on "Ko-Ko" contains a complex harmonic vocabulary (both stated and implied), some styles of playing are based on simpler harmonies and a much slower harmonic rhythm. Many of the early "modal" tunes of the sixties, for example, contain only one or two chords, often radically altering the soloist's approach to melodic patterns.

Instead of relying on the harmonic background to help provide varied tension and relaxation levels, improvisers of the modal style depend on the tension and relaxation tendencies of individual pitches of the mode. Consequently, modal melodic patterns (particularly those in the earliest recordings) tend to remain within the pitches of the mode. Here, the importance of specific scale degrees is often emphasized through repetition of rhythmic alteration rather than through nonchord or nonscale tones.

An example of a masterly treatment, playing on one chord (Dorian mode), is shown in figure 14.2.

Figure 14.2

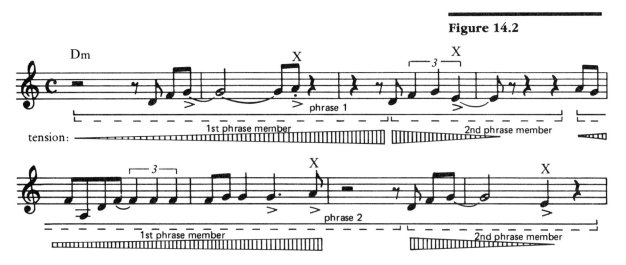

SO WHAT by John Coltrane

The pitch G (measure 1), because of its length and metric placement, establishes the accent phrase and provides the first tension factor. The target note A (next note) increases the tension even through the silence that follows. The next phrase member (measure 2) begins with the same three pitches, rhythmically altered, as the first phrase member then descends to the second scale degree.

This first phrase demonstrates the independence of scale degrees moving over a static harmony. Although the target note A is a chord tone, usually implying relaxation, it functions instead as the dominant of the scale and provides even more tension than the second target note E, a nonchord tone.

The function of each scale degree can be manipulated through the use of rhythm and accent. While in measures 1 and 2 the first phrase member moves briskly from D to A, the second phrase contains a number of delaying tactics, especially for F (measure 5) and G (measure 6)— both are delayed through repetition. Thus, the movement from D to A in the second phrase is extended. Extensions of a line through longer durations tend to lessen the tension or increase it, depending on the position of the target note. The first phrase member of the second phrase (measures 5–6) creates more tension than the corresponding first phrase material because of the extended approach toward a tension pitch. Also, note that the duration of the accent motive (G to A in the third and fourth melodic pitches) has been cut in half in the second phrase (measure 6). Similarly, the extension of the second phrase member (measures 7–8) promotes more relaxation than its corresponding section of the first phrase because of its movement toward a more relaxed rhythmic placement of the pitch E.

Assignment 2

1. Listen to the form of "So What" (*Smithsonian* 11:3). Note the number of measures between the chord change a half step higher (lower).
2. Improvise on the form using Coltrane's solo excerpt as a model.

Melodies Derived from Motivic Structure

The importance of rhythmic structure in the formation of melodic patterns has been discussed in earlier chapters. In this chapter, we have examined melodic patterns based on (1) a harmonic structure and (2) a scale structure. Finally, we must observe melodic patterns based on the combination of harmonic and scale structure on which a higher order has been superimposed. This higher order is motivic relationships.

The Coltrane solo excerpt (fig. 14.2) demonstrates the stretching out of a few basic pitches to accommodate desired tension and relaxation relationships. Now, figure 14.3 illustrates the transfer of an entire motive to another pitch level, regardless of its relationship to the accompanying harmonic background.

In contrast to "So What," "Stolen Moments" is based on a C Dorian blues and therefore contains an obvious harmonic progression. Harmonic implications are immediately apparent in the first six pitches of the solo. However, what first appears to be functional harmony later proves to be an expansion of the motivic framework of those same six pitches. The motive remains at the same pitch level throughout the first three measures. The A♭ of the fourth measure, nevertheless, departs from

Figure 14.3

the scale in order to keep intact the movement of the motive in an ascending fourth progression. The motive expands in the fifth and sixth measures, but near the end reverts to its original form (measure 8). Measure 8 also introduces another pitch from outside the C Dorian mode— Gb. Throughout the twelve bars, the motive has subtly appeared in different parts of measures, still maintaining its original character. Rather than a transformation of a motive (into something somewhat different) such as occurred in the Coltrane example, Oliver Nelson chooses to keep durations basically intact in his solo and simply expand intervallically or change (transpose) to a different pitch level.

Using the twelve-bar progression from figure 14.3, play an improvised solo based upon intervallic transposition. (Play Nelson's solo excerpt *first*.)

Assignment 3

The characteristics of a melodic pattern can differ markedly, depending upon: the structure of the original tune; the style of the individual performer; and to some extent, the collective backgrounds of the supportive musicians (i.e., the rhythm section or style of arrangement). All of these elements taken together, of course, help to define style in a larger sense—concepts vital to the developing improviser.

Today's performers must be prepared for anything—to improvise over a funk beat, a bossa nova rhythm, or a walking bass. Typical of the jazz tradition, moreover, these stylistic techniques are often combined, either written into the tune, as in "Night in Tunisia," or exploited by the group "sound" (Air or Weather Report). Consequently, the performer's choice of melodic patterns most often reflects the style of the music overlaid by an individual, personal statement.

Assignment 4

Transcribe the first sixteen bars of John Coltrane's solo on "Alabama" (*Smithsonian* 12:4). Compare his melodic lines with the excerpt from "So What," which was notated in figure 14.2.

Assignment 5

Trace the development of Ornette Coleman's melodic line through the first nineteen measures of his solo on "Congeniality" (*Smithsonian* 12:2), which has been developed from melodic patterns of the first seven measures.

Summary

The style of an improvised melody reflects both the personal statements of the player as well as influences from the jazz tradition. Improvised melodies can be derived from (1) the harmonic structure, (2) the scale structure, and (3) motivic structure. In all instances, in addition to standard variation techniques (as discussed in chapter 8), the improviser strives to create new and original melodic relationships.

Summary Activity

The first five measures of Charlie Parker's solo on "Embraceable You" (*Smithsonian* 7:8) follow. The first phrase of the original melody is also reproduced.

Parker's motive in measure 1 resembles the first phrase of the original melody only obliquely. (Note, however, that his motive incorporates almost an exact retrograde—is played backwards—of the original tune's first phrase.)

Transcribe a chorus, or part of a chorus, from a solo of an instrument *other* than your own, and trace its development, whether it is derived from a scale, chord, or motivic structure. Analyze as shown in the following example, then play it with the recording.

Scale Substitutions and Combinations

15

Scales, as well as chords, can be substituted for one another. Depending on the melodic effect desired, a particular scale can be transformed from its original structure into a variety of permutations (patterned alterations). Three general types of scale substitutions exist:

1. The use of the same pitches with a substitute tonal center
2. The use of altered scale pitches
3. The addition or deletion of pitches from the original scale

These alterations are present to some degree in all styles of jazz, although in particular styles certain specific types are more prevalent than others. In each instance, however, the choice of scale permutation is governed by one of three functions in the melodic-harmonic framework:

1. Dominant function
2. Tonic function
3. Traveling function

Use of the Same Pitches with a Substitute Tonal Center

In its simplest form, this concept describes the arrangement of scale pitches around a temporary tonic that denotes a desired tension-relaxation relationship with the original key center. As previously described, the scale patterns for the ii–V–I progression are

1. ii = accompanied by scale patterns in the Dorian mode
2. V = accompanied by scale patterns in the Mixolydian mode
3. I = accompanied by scale patterns in the Major mode

All of these scale patterns contain the same pitches, but they are simply rearranged to fit the desired function within the key. Thus, the Dorian mode, through harmonic implications of the ascending-fourth progression, requires movement or "travel" to the Mixolydian mode and eventually the major scale. In addition to this, the tonal tendencies in each of the three modes or scales help establish specific musical effects or "flavors." Especially interesting is the direction of the half-step resolutions in each of the ii–V–I arrangements of the scale (fig. 15.1).

Figure 15.1

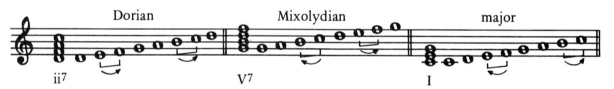

Half steps resolve in the direction of the arrow

Although the pitches forming half steps (E to F and B to C) remain the same in all three scales, their direction of resolution is different in each instance. The Dorian mode deserves its traveling reputation since both half steps resolve in the same direction (up), and in the framework of the C-major tonal center, each succeeding scale degree propels itself upward to the next D (preparing to break away to a scale with dominant function). Mixolydian, on the other hand, resolves its half steps in opposite directions, as does the major scale. However, the Mixolydian resolves to a tritone (B and F), giving it the dominant, or tension, function; whereas the major scale half steps resolve into a consonant interval (E and C), a minor sixth.

Therefore, while many different functions can be formulated from the same original pitches, the means by which these can be accomplished rest both on the relationship of the temporary tonics to the original key center and the resolution direction of the half-step intervals.

To illustrate this point, in C major a Locrian scale (B to B on the white keys of the piano) can be substituted for the Mixolydian (G to G). This alternate scale can be used not only because of its relationship to C, but also because of the resolution direction of its half steps— identical with those of the Mixolydian mode.

Figure 15.2

Substitution of Locrian or Lydian for Mixolydian

Half-steps of both modes resolve in same direction

In the so-called common practice period of jazz, the ii–V–I progression often moves by so quickly that the ii–V relationship becomes compressed. In modal jazz style, however, a complete solo might be based on one Dorian mode, so that the following three sets of relationships become important:

1. The resolution directions of half steps (E to F and B to C in the Dorian mode on D).
2. The whole-step relationships lying adjacent to one another (F, G, A, and B in the Dorian mode on D).
3. The relationship of each pitch of the mode to the tonal center (D in the Dorian mode on D).

Similarly, the pentatonic (five-note) scale, while devoid of half steps, can assume a variety of subtle alterations depending on which of its pitches is used as a temporary tonic (see fig. 15.3).

Figure 15.3

Pentatonic forms

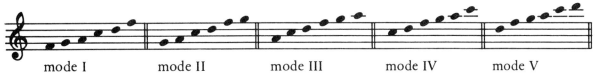

mode I   mode II   mode III   mode IV   mode V

All modes contain the same pitches

While various labels have been used to define the forms of this scale, the first note of any one of these forms, in actual practice, can be given tonic status. The remaining forms (modes) can be used as complementary or temporary dominant regions to explore.

While the scales in figure 15.3 are all arrangements of the same scale pitches, other scales can be constructed that are not simply substitutions of scale order but contain altered pitches to increase tension levels.

The Use of Altered Scale Pitches

The rearrangement of scale pitches, as well as their alteration, is present throughout the history of world musics. The various forms of the minor scale (natural, harmonic, and melodic) in the European tradition, for example, point out this tradition most vividly.

The raised leading tone, first employed to provide sharper tension between tones 7 and 8 in vocal music of the medieval period, eventually evolved into the major and minor scale systems used as a basis of jazz playing today. The proliferation of new, artificial scales since the bebop period has often bewildered performers. In an attempt to insert one exotic scale after another into their solos, improvisers often lose track of the very structure of the composition. Perhaps the solution to this problem lies in the statement above concerning the raised leading tone in the medieval period. The direction of half-step resolution in scales sharing the same pitches, explored above, becomes even more important in the construction and use of scales with altered tones. In the final analysis, the selection of an altered scale is determined by its adherence to the harmonic and melodic tendencies within the phrase.

An altered scale is often used to increase tension; therefore, it is frequently built on the dominant or dominant substitute of the original key. The so-called Lydian dominant, a substitute for Mixolydian, is intensified by adding a raised fourth (C♯ in the key of C major) that resolves up a half step with considerable tension (see fig. 15.4).

Figure 15.4

Comparison of Mixolydian with Lydian dominant

By raising C to C♯, the inner structure of the scale (Mixolydian) is altered to emphasize the fifth (D).

Once an altered scale has been formed, it can be exploited as a confrontation between the original scale and its derived modal configurations (see fig. 15.5).

Figure 15.5

Lydian dominant derivatives

Although all of these altered scales have been labeled in different ways in the past, most improvisers will produce best results by listening to the half-step relationships and their direction of resolution. Trying to remember a group of complicated names, often meaningless, usually generates confusion and creates disorganized improvisation.

The raised fourth scale degree of a Lydian dominant scale is only one of the many altered dominant possibilities. Adding a lowered sixth to a Mixolydian scale would produce the same tension effect as a raised fourth, but the resolution direction would change. It is also possible to combine two scales, both of which have dominant function. For example, a complex group of relationships can be distilled from the use of a dominant functioning scale (like a Mixolydian on G) simultaneous with its tritone substitution (a Mixolydian scale on D♭).

The Addition and Deletion of Scale Pitches

The scale used for the dominant seventh chord in C major can be either G Mixolydian or its tritone substitution, D♭ Mixolydian. Of course, if both scales are used simultaneously with no deleted pitches, the chromatic scale will result (see fig. 15.6).

Figure 15.6

G Mixolydian and tritone substitution—D♭ Mixolydian

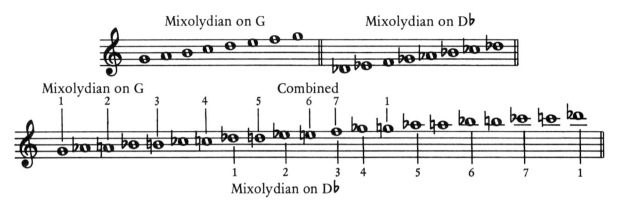

However, if the two dominant seventh chords are extracted from the scales, the following relationships occur (see fig. 15.7).

Figure 15.7

Dominant sevenths from Mixolydian scales

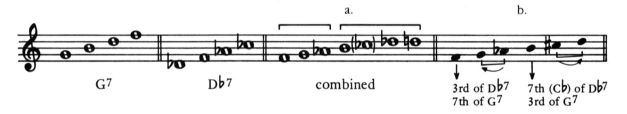

Note that in any arrangement of these six pitches shown in figure 15.7, the half-step resolution is always in the same direction—toward the dominant (G) and its fifth (D).

The combination of both chords comprises a six-tone scale made up of two equal three-note groups. However, with the addition of the sixth degree of both scales, the whole-step-diminished scale results. And, if the fifth of each scale is raised a half step, the whole tone scale is produced (see fig. 15.8).

Figure 15.8

Combinations possible from Mixolydian scales a tritone apart

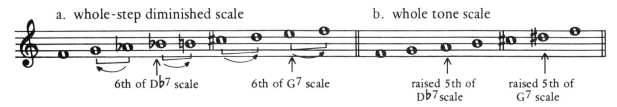

Other less familiar but interesting arrangements of this scale combination are listed below in figure 15.9. The first half of figure 15.9 illustrates the addition of the second of each scale, and the second half illustrates the rearrangement of the same pitches, depicting another form of the same scale.

Figure 15.9

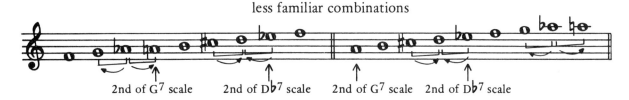

The examples (fig. 15.9) showing the combination of the basic pitches from two scales with various added or deleted tones, can all be substituted for G Mixolydian. Although some pitches have been subtracted, added, or altered in producing new but related scales, some relationships remain constant:

1. From all pitches of the chromatic scale (fig. 15.6), the most important, characterizing the dominant function, remain.
2. While some of the pitches have been altered, the original roots and their tritones (B and F here) have been left intact, and the resolution tendencies of the half steps never wander from their original Mixolydian base.

3. In one instance, (fig. 15.8), the substitution of raised fifths results in a whole-tone scale containing no half steps. Closer scrutiny, however, reveals that even without half-step resolutions, the F whole-tone scale still exemplifies dominant function. This dominant function results because the tritone tension found in the dominant seventh chord is expanded (in the whole-tone scale) to include *all* intervals of a fourth or fifth (which are replaced by tritones).

To summarize, the examples demonstrate that *any* scale pitches might be used with any others so long as structural pitches that identify the function of the scale are used as resolution notes or as basic intervallic material. Since altered scales usually have a dominant function, the original dominant scale or its tritone substitute most often form the basic resolution pitches around which various half steps can be inserted.

Assignment 1

Analyze the scales that follow as dominant functioning in the key of F major. Note resolution pitch directions and, more basically, the structural scale pitches as distinguished from the added or altered tones. The labels given to the following scales constitute points of reference only.

1. (Superlocrian) 2. (Hungarian major) 3. (Enigmatic)

4. (Prometheus) 5. (Prometheus Neapolitan)

Seldom does a performer rely upon one scale formation for a long period of time. Instead, a basic scale is often selected with one or two notes from outside the scale (used as color pitches), finally resolving to scale pitches later in the phrase (see fig. 15.10).

Use of Nonscale pitches and their resolution
Coltrane: end of final chorus of "Blue Train" (*Blue Note,* BST
81577)

Figure 15.10

BLUE TRAIN by John Coltrane.

Beat 1 suggests that the scale used might be the Lydian dominant beginning on C (because of the F♯). However, in beat 2, the function of
F♯ becomes clear—it is a color pitch from outside the C Mixolydian scale
and resolves to G (beat 2). This is confirmed by the presence of the F♮
later in the beat. Similarly, the chromatic descent from D♭ enhances the
root of the C Mixolydian scale. B♮ likewise adorns the seventh (B♭) at
the beginning of beat 4.

Scale pitches can be substituted for one another only mo-
mentarily—before resolving to a functional scale degree. This occurs
not only in the prevailing dominant functioning scale constructions but
is perhaps most frequent in both tonic and traveling function scale formations. Improvisers rarely alter pitches relating to the tonic function.
Temporary alterations of the traveling scale constructions usually anticipate pitches related to the basic *dominant* scale (Mixolydian) through
the half-step approach. A progression, Dm7 to G7, for example, might
include the Dorian beginning on D with an altered tone, A♭, which resolves down to the G (the tonal center of G Mixolydian).

Find examples from a recording in your own collection that contain a
solo line (excerpt) including material based on the dominant. Then:

1. Write out the solo line.
2. Analyze the excerpt to determine whether an altered or substitute
   scale is being used, or whether color pitches are added and then
   resolved within a traditional dominant functioning scale.

Assignment 2

Construct exercise patterns that pertain to the scales used in this chapter. Play in all keys.

Assignment 3

Summary

Substitute scales can be grouped into three classes:

1. The use of the same pitches as the original scale with a substitute tonic
2. The use of altered scale pitches
3. The addition or deletion of pitches from the original scale

Their choice is governed by (1) dominant, (2) tonic, or (3) traveling function in the melodic-harmonic framework.

Voicing and Alteration

Any discussion of chord progression must ultimately include an explanation of voice leading principles. Although voicing can become a complex problem with a variety of alternative solutions (depending on style and instrumentation), only two basic considerations apply:

1. The arrangement of notes (voicing) of each chord and its relation to the next. Included are position (root, first inversion, etc.), spacing, and doubled notes.
2. The resolution of chord pitches according to their own tendencies.

Voicing of a Single Chord

The determination of chord voicing, or "weight," might initially seem to concern only the arranger or a member of the rhythm section rather than the improviser. Nevertheless, the solo line reflects the weight (arrangement) of a chord, through its arrangement of chord tones, as surely as the voicing furnished by a pianist who is comping (see fig. 16.1).

Figure 16.1

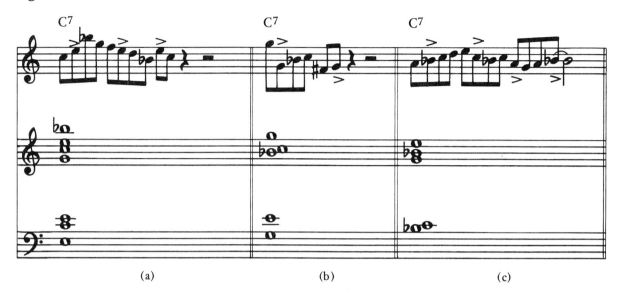

(a)   (b)   (c)

In figure 16.1 (a), note that the improvised line and chord emphasize E. This weight shifts to G in (b) because of the accents, different inversion, and the doubled tones. In (c) the emphasis is on B♭, the spacing between the lowest pitches is compacted, and the third inversion placement brings the two outer voices even more closely together. The lower voices change from an octave (plus sixth) in (a) to a sixth in (b) and to a second in (c).

After the desired voicing is established, each individual voice must move to its closest resolution tone. For example, a V–I progression in F major, moving from tension to relaxation, should reflect this tendency melodically. The seventh (B♭) of the V7 (C7) should resolve down to its relaxation pitch (A) as shown in figure 16.2.

Figure 16.2

F M :   V7   I

In short, after the desired harmonic structure has become established, voicing becomes the melodic treatment of all individual lines, simultaneously.

Resolution of Nonchord Tones in Dominant-Tonic Progression

While voicing can be effective using only diatonic chord tones, the broad concept of voice leading includes nonharmonic tones used as special stress points within the phrase. The voicing of altered and nonchord tones has been purposely delayed until this chapter because the function of the basic harmonic structure must be clearly understood before harmonic alterations can be used efficiently.

The most frequent nonharmonic tones are those a half step away from a resolution pitch. The nonchord tone and its resolution pitch may occur within the same chord or one immediately following. In figure 16.3 (a) a dominant chord anticipates the root of the succeeding chord as its resolution pitch.

Figure 16.3

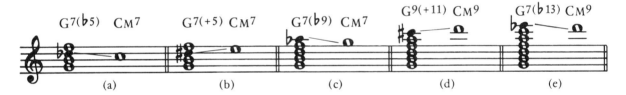

Note that the altered tones in figure 16.3 (a), (b), and (c), resolve to pitches of the C (tonic) *triad,* whereas greater tension is produced in (d) and (e) through resolution to a tonic ninth chord.

Voicing an Eleventh Chord

Altered notes in an extended chord create a high level of tension when all factors are present. Thus, improvisers can regulate the dissonance level by retaining or omitting diatonic notes depending on the effect needed at the moment (see fig. 16.4).

Figure 16.4

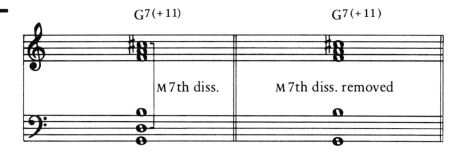

In figure 16.4, the eleventh chord may be voiced to produce a high level of tension or, to reduce the tension, the fifth factor may be eliminated altogether. Thus, tension is regulated by the two basic voicing concepts:

1. The arrangement of the chord (involving close or open position, spacing, and doubling)
2. The resolution of melodic pitches according to natural tendencies (Remember that each "voice" of a chord is considered a melodic note with its own individual tendency for resolution.)

Assignment 1

First, *play* the progressions that follow. Then, answer the questions. For each progression that follows, supply appropriate chord symbols. Determine if specific pitches have been given extra weight (emphasis).
1. Are any chord tones eliminated?
2. Do any of the chords contain altered pitches?
3. What is the effect when small intervals are clustered in the low register? Note (3).
4. What is the effect when small intervals are clustered in the high register? Note (2).
5. Do the tones resolve appropriately in each chord progression?

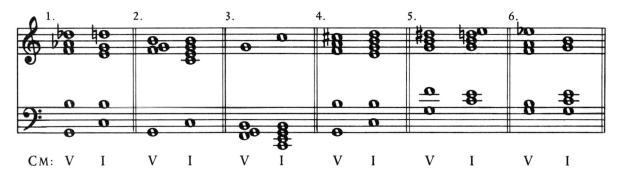

Arrange these chords for various instruments in the class. Play in different ways to judge the effect of timbre on particular voicings.

Write an arrangement for four saxes, trumpet, and trombone using block chords (include altered and extended pitches) moving by half notes through a twelve-bar blues progression.

Voicings Based on Intervals

While the linear aspects of voice leading have been stressed up to this point, a very musical effect (sometimes called *planing* or *parallel chords*) can be created by moving chords in blocks with all voices proceeding in the same direction. When this is done, normal resolutions are often denied and the voicing of chords may be approached through *harmonic* intervals—pairing, for instance, the minor seventh or major seventh.

Figure 16.5

Interval pairing in planed chords

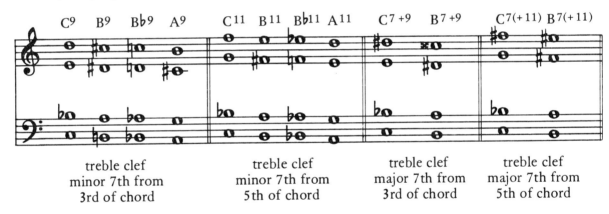

treble clef
minor 7th from
3rd of chord

treble clef
minor 7th from
5th of chord

treble clef
major 7th from
3rd of chord

treble clef
major 7th from
5th of chord

In figure 16.5, the root is not only present, but it also appears as the bass note each time, providing a well-balanced sonority despite the relatively large intervallic distances. Note also that in each example the arrangement of the first chord is carried through the remaining three.

If dominant chords of less stability are desired, a rootless voicing might be preferred. Figure 16.6 demonstrates the use of a stacked tritone plus perfect fourth, using the same harmonic progression as outlined in figure 16.5.

Figure 16.6

Dominant chords of less stability

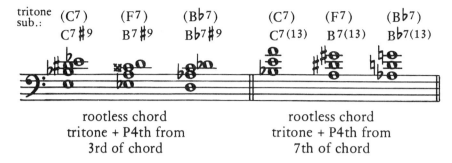

rootless chord
tritone + P4th from
3rd of chord

rootless chord
tritone + P4th from
7th of chord

Figure 16.6 illustrates the tritone and perfect fourth combination built from the third and seventh. Not only can the second chord in each example be interchanged with its tritone substitute (F7–B7), but the remainder of the chords are also similarly interchangeable. The first chord, C7, begins on the third, which could be interpreted as the seventh of F♯7; B♭ enharmonically spelled becomes A♯ (the third of F♯7); and, D♯ is the thirteenth of F♯7.

While figures 16.5 and 16.6 contain both root position and rootless voicings of dominant harmonies, the following figures will include ii–V–I progressions voiced with combinations of triads plus fourths and triads plus tritones. Figure 16.7 illustrates the basic triad (ii) in the outer voices with perfect fourths or tritones in the middle. The roots are present in these chords although in figure 16.7 (b) rootless voicings appear in combination with perfect fifth and major third, with the tritone and perfect fourth, and with stacked perfect fourths.

Figure 16.7

Triads with P5/M3, T/4th, and stacked P4ths

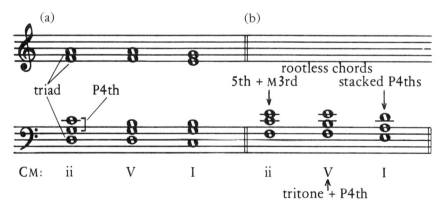

The use of stacked fourths (known as **quartal harmony**) in the tonic triad (fig. 16.7, b) is especially useful in modal playing. The ambiguity of superimposed fourths can be increased or decreased by selecting lower factors (root, third, fifth) or higher factors (seventh, ninth, eleventh, thirteenth) as the basic note. Some of the most effective quartal harmonies in a ii–V–I progression appear in figure 16.8.

Figure 16.8

Effective quartal harmonies

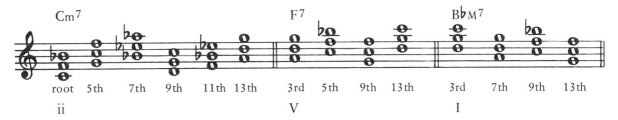

Notice in figure 16.8 that some pitches of the thirteenth chord are not used as roots. No structure is built from the third of the Cm7 chord because the result (Eb Ab Db) is too far removed from the original (C Eb G Bb) or Bb major scale—the only note in common is the Eb. Some quartal chords, however, serve more than one function. G C F is related to the Cm7, F7, or Bb M7 chords. Superimposed (one on top of the other) fourths are occasionally found in combination (see fig. 16.9).

Figure 16.9

Quartal chords superimposed

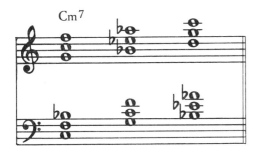

Interesting effects can also be obtained from other intervals in combination with fourths.

Figure 16.10

Other intervals in combination with fourths

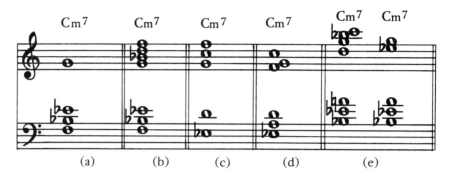

(a)   (b)   (c)   (d)   (e)

a. Superimposed fourths plus M3— "So What" voicing.
b. Same as (a) except that a seventh chord is built above the note G.
c. A combination of seventh and fourths.
d. A basic quartal (tritone as bottom fourth) combination with added second—the note F.
e. A combination of P4 A4 with doubled tone—the note E♭.

Assignment 3   Play quartal harmonies related to ii–V–I progressions.

Next, play combinations of superimposed fourths (both perfect and augmented) with added thirds, fifths, or sevenths.

Whereas chords built from thirds are usually constructed to provide a clear definition of diatonic structure, quartal harmonies tend to blur the underlying function. Chords built by superimposing seconds are also possible, but in the jazz idiom are usually added to the existing harmonic framework.

Figure 16.11

Chords in seconds added to existing harmony

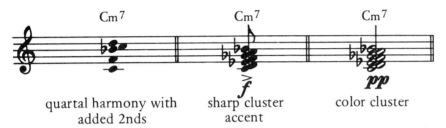

quartal harmony with   sharp cluster   color cluster
added 2nds   accent

Voicings based on interval combinations can also be extended to include triad combinations. These are known as **polychords.** In order to project the presence of two different triads, it is important to delineate the two triads by spacing them some distance apart. It is also helpful to voice the lower triad in open position, thus allowing its overtones to identify with matching pitches from the upper triad.

Figure 16.12

Superimposed triads—polychords

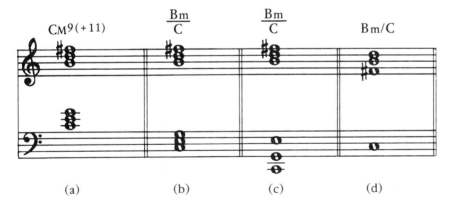

(a)   (b)   (c)   (d)

a. Functions as *one* chord—CM9 (+11) rather than as two triads. The chords are not far enough apart, and the two together form a single, more recognizable chord.

b. Two triads are present, but the intervals in the lower triad are voiced so close in a low register that the sound is unclear and cannot blend in a composite sound.

c. This produces a true polychord sound and is well spaced.

d. This is simply a Bm triad with a C pedal tone.

Arrangers are often unclear in their symbology, whether they call for a pedal tone, a polychord, or simply a chord extension. The straight line (illustrated below) indicates a polychord (two chords) while the slash (/) refers to a pedal tone.

Polychord   Pedal Tone

Bm   Bm/C
———
C

If there is a special weight (emphasis) to be given to one or two pitches or an unusual spacing, *all* pitches should be notated for as long as the special voicing exists.

Assignment 4

1. Play the following ii–V–I progressions at the keyboard.
2. Discuss the various voicing combinations.
3. Add several more voicing illustrations of your own.

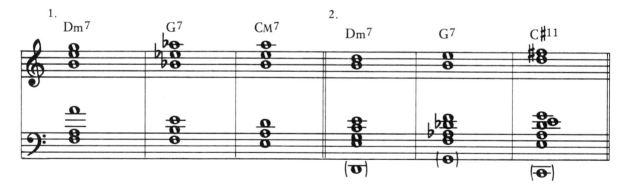

3.

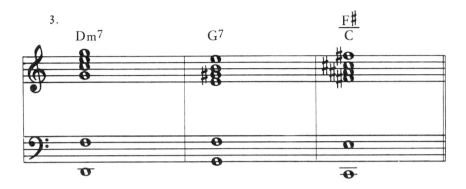

Listen to "Summertime" recorded by Miles Davis (*Smithsonian* 10:2), and note the register in which Gil Evans places the background horns behind the trumpet solo. Imagine how the line would have sounded if played by trombones in their low register. Then, listen to the head of "In a Mellowtone" by Duke Ellington (*Smithsonian* 7:1), and discuss how Ellington effectively uses different registers and voicings between melody and accompaniment. How does he provide contrasts later in the arrangement?

Assignment 5

From the accompanying cassette recording, write the chord progression played behind Interval Dictations 1, 2, 3, and 4 in Appendix III. Note that the progression remains the same in all four examples while the melody and tempo change each time.

Assignment 6

Play ascending perfect fourth and ascending perfect fifth progressions from the accompanying ii–V cassette recording (notation in Appendix IV).

Assignment 7

Construct appropriate voicing exercises to play at the keyboard to accompany the ii–V recording (Appendix IV).

Assignment 8

Summary

Concepts of chord construction and progression must ultimately include principles of voice leading: the arrangement of the notes of a single chord and the movement of each individual note toward the next. Chord tones and nonchord tones usually move in the direction of their individual tendencies, usually a half step or whole step away. Other possibilities include the parallel movement of one block chord to another, with all voices moving in the same direction. The construction of such chords is often based on the superimposition of specific intervals, such as sevenths, fourths, or seconds.

Summary Activity

Play "My Funny Valentine," which follows, then:

1. Write out and perform a piano harmonization (use half or whole notes) while another class member plays the melodic line.
2. On your own instrument, improvise on the chord changes you have written, providing the desired "weight" of the harmony through your melodic line.

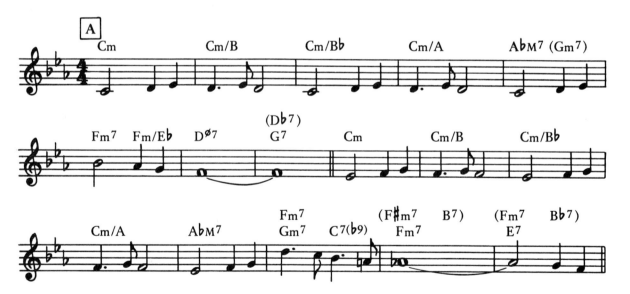

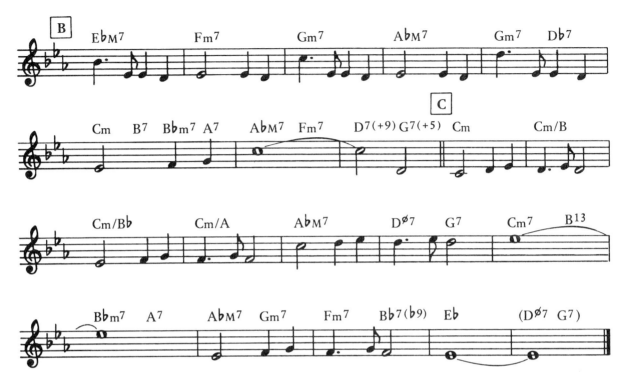

MY FUNNY VALENTINE, from "Babes in Arms." Music by Richard Rodgers, words by Lorenz Hart. Copyright © 1937 by Chappell & Co., Inc.
Copyright renewed. International Copyright Secured. ALL RIGHTS RESERVED. Used by permission.

Scales, Chords, Motives, and Harmonic Rhythm

17

The relationships between vertical (chords) and horizontal (melody) pitches can be approached in any of the following ways:

1. The *chord* selection influences the *scale* to be used.
2. The *scale* selection influences the *chord* to be used.
3. Combine 1 and 2 in a higher structural order.

Chord to Scale Approach

In the chord-to-scale technique, a particular chord cues the melodic improviser to select a matching scale. Thus, when the ii chord is heard, the performer automatically selects the Dorian mode. When the V chord appears, the Mixolydian scale is suggested, and so on. If a chord is altered to express higher tension, the scale must reinforce this alteration and employ the same modifications. Thus, if a C7 chord is altered to include a +5, the improviser will traditionally select the C whole-tone scale. Similarly, a C7(+11) suggests the Lydian dominant scale.

Figure 17.1

Altered chords with matching scales

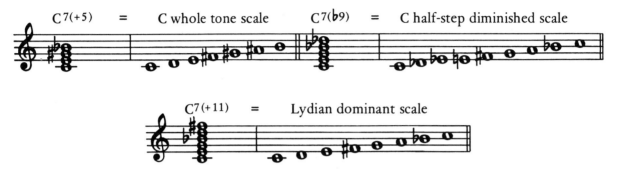

While extended (ninth, eleventh, and thirteenth) chords reflect the pitches of the scale to be stressed, altered chords provide new color tones, higher tension, and the opportunity for a variety of different scales. As is shown in figure 17.1, all three scales provide dominant function in F major.

Scale to Chord Approach

The scale-to-chord method also provides an opportunity to observe relationships between the vertical and linear aspects of improvisation. Just as the improviser must adjust major scale pitches to reflect dominant, tonic, or traveling function, these same functions, particularly with altered pitches, can also be served through the formation of tetrachords that become structurally important.

Melodically, the half step, as part of a tetrachord, represents tension and relaxation capabilities comparable to that of the harmonic progression, dominant to tonic. In contrast, a whole step in a tetrachord represents traveling function similar to that of a ii, iii, or vi chord. A tetrachord containing only half steps nullifies any tendencies, while exclusive use of whole steps projects a dominant function.

Below, the GAB♭C tetrachord provides either tonic or dominant function depending on the direction of the half-step resolution.

Figure 17.2

Resolution of half steps

Motivic Approach

If we look at the relationship of chords vs. melody in a slightly different way, the pitches of a tetrachord (or even larger scale unit) can also combine with chord pitches to produce organization at a higher level. The GAB♭C tetrachord, for example, consists of the 1–3–7–9 factors of the A7(♭9) chord. Not only does this tetrachord match the chord notes, but it can also provide an interesting motivic nucleus for solo improvisation.

Figure 17.3 illustrates the use of a tetrachord along with a sequence (short figure repeated at a different pitch). For the improviser, employing sequences is a basic technique for extending material, providing direction for a longer span of melody, and creating a smooth line. Note that not only does each section of the sequence maintain similar pitch relationships, but the first note of each of the three sections plus the very last note comprise an inversion of the original tetrachord (GFED♭).

Figure 17.3

Tetrachord with sequence

Motivic construction, such as that illustrated in figure 17.3, can of course be extended to include larger intervals, or contracted to produce even smaller ones. The important point to remember here is that both continuity and coherence are most easily maintained through the use of short motives (like tetrachords). With these smaller units, tendency tones are more easily recognized and the desired shape of the improvised solo can be more clearly fashioned.

The Relationship between Motives and Scales

The connection of a motive to its repetition, expansion, or contraction can be made through pitches of the scale that are related to the prevailing chord. In figure 17.4, the chord is A7, so that the related scale is A Mixolydian. The tetrachord motive itself is not related to Mixolydian, but by filling out the octave with notes of the Mixolydian, connections between improvised forms of the motive can be made skillfully and smoothly. The basic Mixolydian scale pitches are used as "filler" notes.

Figure 17.4

Connecting forms of a motive with scale pitches

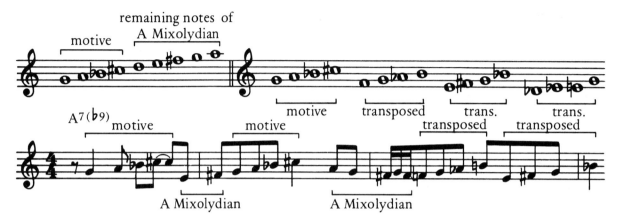

The importance of structural melodic notes either as separate pitches uniting a phrase or combined to form a motive as described here cannot be overemphasized. The length of filler material may vary depending on the personal style and taste of the performer. Inexperienced improvisers tend to play too many rather than too few filler notes.

While the A7(♭9) from figures 17.3 and 17.4 might traditionally derive melodic material from the A *half-step diminished scale*, a tetrachord (GAB♭C♯) combined with the remaining pitches of the A Mixolydian scale provides interesting new scale colors.

Figure 17.5

New scales derived from tetrachord and Mixolydian scale

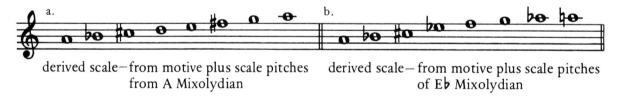

derived scale—from motive plus scale pitches
from A Mixolydian

derived scale—from motive plus scale pitches
of E♭ Mixolydian

Assignment 1

1. The instructor plays one of the following chords.
2. A class member immediately plays a conjunct (stepwise) ascending tetrachord beginning on A that agrees with the chord (contains at least two notes found in the chord).
3. Continue through all the following chords in the manner described in 2. Then using the same chords, complete the following:

a. Student plays a *descending* stepwise tetrachord beginning on A that agrees with the chord (contains at least two notes found in the chord).
b. Student plays a motive based on the tetrachord.
c. Student plays a complete scale based on the notes of the chord.

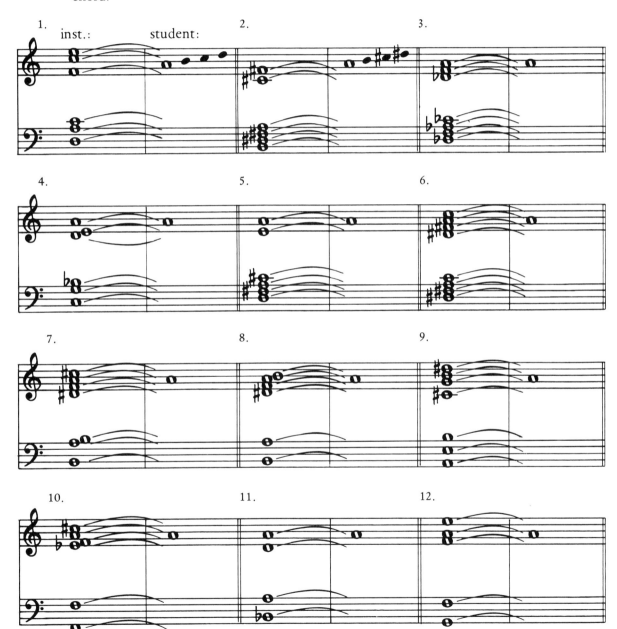

Assignment 2

1. The instructor plays one of the following scales.
2. Members of the class who play harmonic instruments then play a seventh, ninth, eleventh, or thirteenth chord (root is D) in no. 1, for example, that agrees with the scale (all chord tones are part of the scale). For those who play melodic instruments, repeat the scale as played, then arpeggiate the chord (beginning on D).
3. Complete all scales using the same procedure.
4. For further practice the following are recommended. After the instructor plays the first scale
   a. play the chord and build a motive from any desired scale pitch (not D).
   b. treat the motive sequentially through all scales and implied chords that follow.

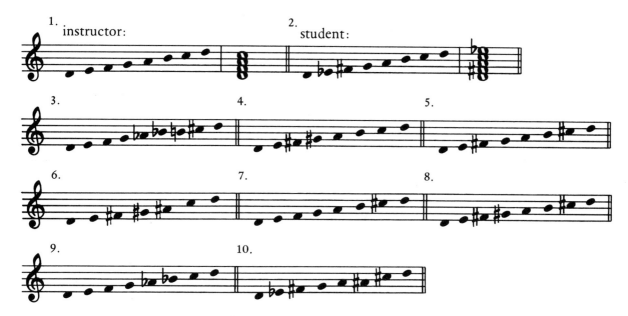

Tendencies always exist for improvisers to concentrate on the chord-to-scale approach (example: horn player reacts to a chord from the rhythm section) or a scale-to-chord method (example: keyboard player listens to a melodic modification by the soloist and adjusts accordingly). These are natural tendencies and result from simple practicalities. However, a performer seldom derives material from *all* notes of a scale (such as major, minor, Dorian, etc.). In many instances, enough time simply does not exist because rapidly changing altered chords require instantaneous matching of these changes in the melody line. One might assume from this that practicing complete scales such as Dorian, Lydian, etc., is unnecessary. But just because of these limitations of time, practicing complete scales is vital and makes it possible to choose any section of a scale when needed.

Harmonic Rhythm

The term **harmonic rhythm** refers to the frequency of harmonic changes in a composition. Thus, a fast harmonic rhythm in 3/4 meter occurs when a different chord is introduced on each beat. If a new chord were introduced only once per measure, the harmonic rhythm would be comparatively slower.

   While greater tension levels can be obtained through altered and extended chords, harmonic rhythm can also contribute. In figure 17.6, the given chords are shown in a. In b the final chord (CM9) is introduced a half beat early, thus providing additional tension. The change of harmonic rhythm produces that tension. In c, the implied harmonic rhythm in the improvised melodic line moves much faster than the given chords (shown above the staff). The result, again, is greater tension produced by a faster harmonic rhythm.

Figure 17.6

Tension produced by harmonic rhythm

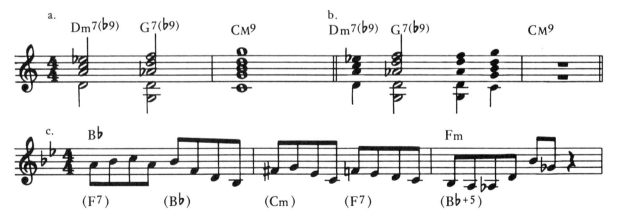

The given harmonic rhythm of a composition may vary from a chord change on every beat to only one throughout an entire section. What the soloist adds to or substracts from a given chord structure, of course, depends somewhat on the style of the piece. Funk-inspired lines often rely on rhythmic placement of only one chord, while bebop lines are more complex harmonically—as shown in figure 17.6 (c).

Such oversimplification can be dangerous, however. A great artist, such as Charlie Parker, is not only able to imply more chords than are given in one phrase (as in the "Ko-Ko" excerpt shown in fig. 17.7, first phrase), but is able to build the tension and relaxation structure on a larger level in his second phrase (fig. 17.7, second phrase). He accomplishes this by reducing his material to a five-note motive without rhythmic variation.

Figure 17.7

KO-KO by Charlie Parker. © 1946 Atlantic Music Corporation. 1974 renewed and assigned © Atlantic Music Corporation. Used by permission.

Assignment 3

Listen to the two versions by Charlie Parker of "Embraceable You" (*Smithsonian* 7:8 and 7:9) to recognize the growth of tension he generated throughout his solos through the harmonic rhythm and changes of motivic ideas. Also, note the material in the second version as contrasted with that of the first.

John Coltrane is also responsible for many new concepts of harmonic rhythm, sometimes by accelerating it and at other times by slowing it. On occasion he does both simultaneously! Coltrane's classic two-chord-per-measure tune, "Giant Steps," is well known for its tonal centers that are a third apart (known as *third relationship*). More conventional tunes contain tonal centers a perfect fourth apart. In figure 17.8, his masterly balance between chord tension and relaxation (two V-to-I progressions in the first three measures), coupled with the ambiguity of the descending major thirds produced by the roots of major seventh chords (measures 1–3) is remarkable. The smoothness of the passage is unusual because of its sequential treatment—the chords in measures 5–7 as well as the melody notes are a sequence of measures 1–3, a major third lower. Therefore, the structure heard in the first three measures is amplified to include the first seven measures. The set of four melody notes in measures 1–3 and its sequence in measures 5–7 is a descending whole-tone scale (B–A–G–F–E♭) and (G–F–E♭–D♭–B). Thus, the seven-measure excerpt contains two resolution points—the melody notes E♭ and B.

Figure 17.8

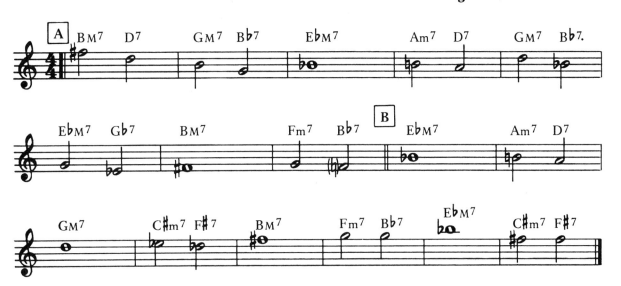

GIANT STEPS by John Coltrane. Copyright Jowcol Music. Used courtesy of Jowcol Music.

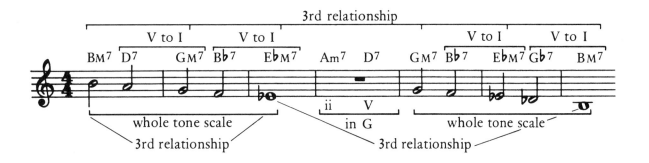

Assignment 4	Play the ascending and descending M and m third ii–V melodies, Appendix IV.

Assignment 5	Play "Giant Steps," first as a ballad, then gradually increase the tempo from performance to performance. *Memorize carefully.*

On the other hand, Coltrane also took the simple harmonic progression from the song, "My Favorite Things" and simplified the progression even further. Working from various target pitches in the scale and over a repeated bass tone (B), Coltrane created a modal flavor and at the same time stretched out the original form of the composition.

During part of his improvisation, Eric Dolphy, in his performance of the same tune with the Coltrane group, not only subscribed to the modal treatment of his peers, but also focused on tones not found in the original scale. Although the original tune is in E minor, Dolphy injected tension into his solo occasionally by building lines around F♮.

More recent performers have slowed down the harmonic rhythm in their compositions while increasing the harmonic rhythm in their solo part. Still others have accomplished an artistic result through opposite means.

Understanding the strategic use of harmonic rhythm, either designated or implied, is of vital importance in fashioning artistic improvisation.

Obviously the goal of any improvisational effort is musical credibility, and this chapter has demonstrated a variety of ways in which this goal can be accomplished. Listening to as many different styles and performers as possible should remain central to the development of any aspiring improviser.

Summary

Melodic and harmonic relationships can be approached in several ways: (1) chord to scale, (2) scale to chord, (3) the combination of (1) and (2) to develop a higher structural order.

Summary Activity

From the *Smithsonian Collection* (9:7), listen to "Smoke Gets in Your Eyes" performed by Thelonious Monk. He first shares the melodic line with the horn players by playing a melodic paraphrase during the head. The first several bars of his solo (after the horn players have finished) is shown in the following excerpt.

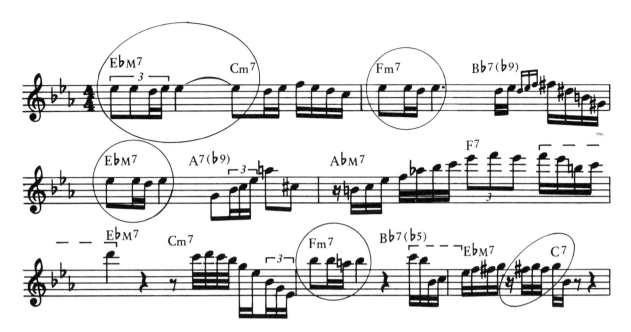

SMOKE GETS IN YOUR EYES by Otto Harbach and Jerome Kern. Copyright © 1933 T. B. Harms Company. Copyright Renewed c/o The Welk Music Group, Santa Monica, CA. 90401. International Copyright Secured. All Rights Reserved. Used by permission.

Monk uses a short motive (circled in the excerpt) as the basis of this solo, with only two pointed references to the original melody (shown in dotted lines). Except for its first and last appearances, the motive retains the same rhythm at the same pitch level and always begins on the first beat of the measure. Although the motive is, in the beginning, the *initiator* of different, supplementary material, its last two appearances occur as a climactic point at the *end* of a phrase section.

Between motivic appearances he alternates between the scale-to-chord and chord-to-scale approach. In measure 1, for example, the last six sixteenth notes encompass 1–4 of the C minor scale, whereas the last four pitches of measure 2 spell out a G♯m7 chord (sounding 7–♭9–11–♭13 of the extended B♭7 chord). The same alternation exists throughout the notated excerpt.

1. Find instances of chord-to-scale and scale-to-chord approaches throughout the notation and, next, throughout the nonnotated remainder of the solo.
2. Transcribe the remainder of the solo and play with the recording.

Recent Forms

Many compositions have been written in new formal structures other than the traditional thirty-two-bar and sixteen-bar forms. Not only have composers used different lengths of compositions but also have initiated different compositional techniques within the sixteen- and thirty-two-bar framework, sometimes in combination with traditional methods. Modal devices, for example, which promote a sense of stasis, have been united with goal-oriented harmonies, which focus on the next functional chord.

Traditionally, however, the composition of new material has never been so important as the improvisation derived from it. Bebop players, for example, often took a popular tune of the twenties or thirties, changed only the melodic line or added some chord changes, while keeping the external form intact. There was no basic conflict between the external and internal structures since both were concerned with growth through harmonic development: the AABA structure of the tunes and the ii–V–I insertions of the bebop players reenforced each other on both the macrolevels and microlevels.

Modal Playing

The writing of new compositions gradually became more important, however, as new ways of thinking about structure emerged—the interior structure began to shape the external structure. Miles Davis's compositions, such as "Milestones" and "Flamenco Sketches," shifted the emphasis from a vertical to a linear approach, leading the way toward modal playing.

For example, "Milestones," an ABA tune of forty measures (16+16+8), focuses on linear elements both harmonically and melodically. There are only two structural chords, Gm7 in the A section and Am7 in the B section. The long duration of each chord, the m7 "traveling" quality of its construction, as well as the root movement in seconds (rather than fourths) bring about a static quality, which negates traditional harmonic function. Similarly, the melody of both the A section and the B section is based upon the same four-note shape, (F–G–A–G). Melodic tension is accomplished only through repetition (in the A section) and through interval contraction and expansion in the B section, as the overall melodic structure remains the same. One structural characteristic, which reflects traditional formal construction, however, is the placement of the B section melody a perfect fourth higher than that of the A section.

Circularity

These structural elements combine to form a characteristic, not only common to modal tunes, but also to many other, newer compositions: **circularity.** The melodic repetition of F–G–A–G–F–G–A, etc., in the A section brings about an equality of each pitch, devoid of structural function. In fact, the last pitch of the section is a G, which finishes the line in midcircle.

In the transition between the fast harmonic rhythms of bebop and the static harmony of modal tunes, both concepts were sometimes joined together. One such tune, which exemplifies circularity as well as innovative linear and vertical combinations, is John Coltrane's "Giant Steps," which he recorded in 1959. Although widely discussed as an example of vertical harmonies, "Giant Steps" also projects a new direction in horizontal root relationships. As mentioned in the previous chapter, Coltrane uses temporary tonics a third apart rather than the traditional ascending fourth. Also, as was pointed out, the first seven measures of the composition move toward only two tonic pitches (despite the presence of six M7 chords), which are harmonized through the ambiguity of whole-tone scale steps.

The same major sevenths are used in the B section of the piece as in the A section. While this adds to the circular quality, their arrangement is in a different order, effecting functional ii–V–I relationships (fig. 18.1).

Figure 18.1

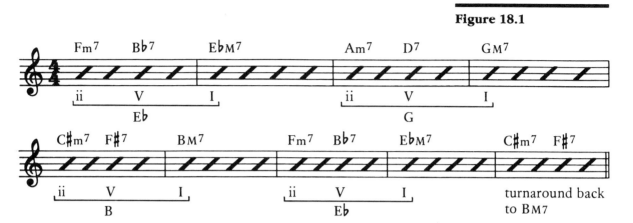

GIANT STEPS by John Coltrane. Copyright Jowcol Music. Used courtesy of Jowcol Music.

Thus, "Giant Steps" combines both a linear emphasis in the A section and a vertical emphasis in the B section. Also, the number of quickly moving chords project a sense of verticality while the recurrences of the same tonics reflect a sense of the horizontal. The overall balance of the form is also irregular: instead of the traditional 8+8 arrangement, the A section is composed of seven measures while the B section consists of nine measures.

Listen to "So What" (*Smithsonian* 11:3). Analyze the tune as to

Assignment 1

1. the number of measures in each section
2. the functional chords and root relationships
3. the melodic structure
4. the use of repetition to effect circularity

Transcribe Miles Davis's solo and play it. According to the criteria above, analyze the solo and point out phrases and sections that emphasize his expression of modal concepts.

Irregular Designs

Many other compositions written since the early sixties also combine modal characteristics with some aspects of earlier tradition. Often this results in an irregular design. For example, instead of an ABA or AAB head followed by solos on the form and a reiteration of the head at the end, a contemporary composer might write an AB, then solos over different changes, followed by an open solo section (no prescribed chords), concluded by an A' section of a different length. This description fits Tony Williams' composition, "Wildlife," for example.

The open solo concept, which allows the performer to devise his or her own formal structure in addition to his or her own melodic and harmonic ideas, certainly emphasizes improvisation as spontaneous composition. The free jazz movement of the sixties not only required each performer to improvise on a broader level but also to interact with other players, thus developing group compositions. Ornette Coleman's composition, "Congeniality" (*Smithsonian* 12:2), is a forerunner of much of the free jazz which was to follow. Coleman's departure from tradition is tempered by a deep respect for it, however. The head is a combination of traditional bebop lines as well as freer sounding melodic unisons ending with a fermata. Although this piece can also be considered to unite both the goal orientation of bebop with the static qualities of modal playing, the same qualities were sometimes present in earlier structures, although to a lesser degree. For example, the introduction to Charlie Parker's "Ko-Ko" recording (before his solo on the "Cherokee" changes) is a microcosm of the structure of the head of "Congeniality." What Coleman did differently was to extend the shapes of the freer sounding material and retain only an implication of traditional harmonic functions.

"Congeniality" contains weakened harmonic functions because of both external and internal factors. The most obvious change is in the makeup of the rhythm section: there is no pianist comping behind the soloists. Internally, however, although the first motive spells a descending minor triad, the structural pitches deflect any resemblance to traditional harmonic function (D–Eb–F in the first phrase). While the pitch centers throughout the piece fluctuate between Eb, E♮, and F, tension and relaxation are accomplished through time relationships (the conflict between rhythmic flow and its suspension) as much as through circular pitch tendencies.

Play the head of "Congeniality" with the record, paying close attention to the exact time relationships.

Assignment 2

Write a tune of your own that you feel exemplifies Coleman's ideas in "Congeniality." (Write the melodic line(s) for horn players and include a written bass line and drum part where needed.)

Assignment 3

Experiments in the time-relationship structure have always been the basis of new style development in jazz music, from the subtle changes in the duration and accents of eighth-note groupings in the thirties and forties to the development of expanded structures based on a rhythmic motive à la Cecil Taylor in the seventies and eighties. The changes in time structures, which resulted from the slowing of harmonic rhythm and the emphasis on linear playing, have made available other time-related concepts, which have permeated all aspects of the music.

The Soloist Complex durational values, irregular meters, irregular changes of harmonic rhythm, irregular lengths of phrases, and free improvisation

The Composition All of the above, plus irregular forms, and rhythms borrowed from other idioms such as rock, funk, and reggae

The Ensemble All of the above, plus changing function of the rhythm section, and group improvisation

Play the blues in the following meters: 3/4, 5/4, 7/4, and 11/4.

Assignment 4

On a given chord, improvise over a rock, funk, or reggae beat. Suggested recordings:

Assignment 5

Rock: Jimi Hendrix, "Are You Experienced?"; "Rush, I"; or "Led Zeppelin, I"

Funk: Bernie Worrell, "Who of the World"; Parliament, "Clones of Dr. Funkenstein," and "Mothership Connection"; Funkadelic, "One Nation under a Groove," and "Tales of Kid Funkadelic"

Reggae: Bob Marley, "Exodus" and "Kaya"; Peter Tosh, "Equal Rights"; or Jimmy Cliff, "The Harder They Come"

The influences on the structure of today's music reach far back into the traditions of stride piano and ragtime as well as the bebop and modal styles, which are more often performed. The results of combining elements from the past with some of the rhythms of recent pop idioms as well as those of contemporary classical music seem to point toward continual experiments with structure, both on a large scale and within the smallest rhythmic units. Perhaps the most extensive loosening of traditional structural elements occurs in free jazz and group improvisation.

As stated earlier, Ornette Coleman was one of the pioneers of free jazz (also the title of an album under his leadership). This concept has undergone many transformations since 1960. For both the soloist and the group participant, one condition remains the same—technically, there is no such thing as "free" improvisation. The combination of traditional elements with new ideas has already been discussed in regard to the Coleman composition "Congeniality," and so it is with the improvisations that followed.

Whether the structure to be improvised upon consists of a specific number of measures without given chords, or an indefinite length of measureless time, improvisers in this new tradition must supply the structure not given by the composer. In a group improvisational setting, the structure is likely to be built from motivic interaction, either rhythmic, melodic, or harmonic. The solo player must interact only with himself or herself, playing on the structure he or she has already presented. This provides a player with opportunities to shape the music in a very personal way but at the same time makes demands on the player's ability to discipline his or her musical ideas to a degree that has not yet been approached in any other playing situation.

An excellent example of "free" improvisation occurs in Cecil Taylor's recording of "Enter Evening" (*Smithsonian* 11:2). The contrast between the shaping of musical material by Taylor and by Roscoe Mitchell in his solo on "Nonaah," (from the album of the same title) points to the degree of flexibility with which an artist can mold structures to fit his or her personal tastes, and at the same time, provide a coherent musical statement through the use of "free" improvisation.

Examples of group improvisation, such as those heard on Mitchell's "Sound" (1966) and in Anthony Braxton's, Archie Shepp's, and Sun Ra's groups of the seventies, all depict individual directions that are being realized in the eighties. One group, which has maintained individual concepts and has yet continually refined group improvisational concepts, is the Art Ensemble of Chicago. Their synthesis of traditional jazz, African rhythms, classical avant-garde, and the blues, points to the importance of each musician's being aware of tradition as well as new music, and the necessity of putting these elements together into a coherent structure, either individually or in a group setting.

Assignment 6

Write a short solo composition for your instrument. From the material you have written, continue improvising in the same vein. Tape it, or play it for the class, and decide whether the composed and improvised material coincide—or collide.

Assignment 7

As a group, improvise on the shape below for three minutes. (How can the basic musical elements—pitch, duration, timbre and intensity—be used to make this structure coherent and musically interesting?)

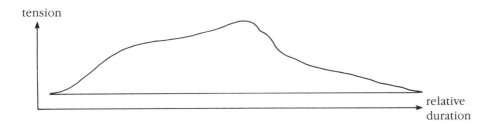

Summary

The shift from a vertical to a horizontal structure in the early sixties brought about radical, new directions in compositional and improvisational structure. Modal playing, circularity, and irregular designs have affected the function of the soloist, the composition, and the ensemble.

Summary Activity

From the following melodic line:

1. Write another section to complement or contrast with the given line.
2. Write chord change(s).
3. Construct a performance design. For example, A (given melody), B (your added section), A (repeated) followed by a variant of the B section is only one of many possibilities.
4. Play in class and discuss the different structures performed by your class members.

Section 3 Summary

Chapter 14. Stylistic Alterations   In addition to influences from the jazz tradition and the personal statements from the player, melodic types can be categorized according to (1) harmonic structure, (2) scale structure, and (3) motivic structure.

Chapter 15. Scale Substitutions and Combinations   Substitute scales are grouped into three categories: (1) the same pitches with substitute tonal centers, (2) altered scale pitches, (3) pitches added to or deleted from the original scale. Their choice is governed by (1) dominant, (2) tonic, or (3) traveling functions in the melodic-harmonic framework.

Chapter 16. Voicing and Alteration   Voicing includes the placement of pitches in one chord as well as the movement of each line, according to its natural tendencies, toward the next harmony. Chords can also be constructed from the superimposition of specific intervals such as sevenths, fourths, or seconds. Often these chords move in parallel blocks—all pitches moving in the same direction.

Chapter 17. Scales, Chords, Motives, and Harmonic Rhythm   Melodic and harmonic relationships can be approached from (1) the chord to the scale, (2) the scale to the chord, (3) the combination of (1) and (2) into a higher structural order.

Chapter 18. Recent Forms   Although the formal structure has traditionally not been so important as the improvisation derived from it, the shift to a linear approach (with the advent of modal playing) has affected both compositional form and the style of improvisation since the sixties.

Summary Activity

Pick one of the compositions you have learned from the book and play it in several different styles (the improvisation style must parallel that of the arrangement).

For example, if you choose to play "My Funny Valentine" (pp. 170–71) you might perform it as follows:

1. Play the melody as written, but use a G (pedal tone) under the harmonies during measures 1–4 and an Ab pedal throughout measures 5–8. During the bridge, use a Bb pedal alternating with a Gm and Ab chord where appropriate. The use of a pedal tone a fifth higher than the tonic root is the procedure used by Coltrane in his modal treatment of "My Favorite Things" mentioned earlier.
2. Devise a line of two measures that constantly repeats (ostinato) against the melody (refer to the ostinato behind Miles Davis's recording of "Summertime").
3. Instead of playing the head followed by solo improvisations, begin with a group improvisation which focuses upon the first motive (measures 1–2). Develop the melodic pattern until the tension has been expanded and contracted—then end the performance with the melodic line in unison (perhaps against the pedal described in step 1).

Discography

A. Style evolution: composition
   1. "Cherokee"
      (a) Charlie Barnet and his Orchestra (*The Big Band Sound*, RCA CC12–0619, e)
      (b) Charlie Parker *(Smithsonian Collection)* or Clifford Brown (*Brownie Eyes*, Applause Records, APBL–2314) listed in the Discography at the end of Section 2)
   2. "Night In Tunisia"
      (a) Charlie Parker (Prestige 24009 in vol. 1 of the *Prestige 24000 Series*)
      (b) Rahsaan Roland Kirk (*Kirkatron*, Warner Bros. Records BS 2982)
   3. "Nonaah"
      (a) The Art Ensemble of Chicago (*Fanfare for the Warriors*, Atlantic FD1651)
      (b) Roscoe Mitchell (*The Roscoe Mitchell Solo Saxophone Concerts*, Sackville 2006)
      (c) Roscoe Mitchell (*Nonaah* [three versions] Nessa n–9/10)
   4. "Epistrophy"
      (a) Thelonious Monk and John Coltrane (*Monk/Trane*, Milestone M–47011)
      (b) Frank Lowe (*Fresh*, Arista AL1075)

B. The present and future: some of the groups and individuals
1. The Art Ensemble of Chicago (*Urban Bushmen,* ECM. GmbH)
2. Jack de Johnette (*Special Edition,* ECM–1–1152)
3. Gerry Hemingway (*Kwambe,* Auricle Records. Aur–1)
4. Rashied Ali, Le Roy Jenkins Duo (*Swift Are the Winds of Life,* Survival SR 112)
5. Dave Holland and Derek Bailey (*Improvisations for Cello and Guitar,* ECM 1013 ST)
6. Roscoe Mitchell and the Sound Ensemble (*3X 4Eye,* Black Saint BSR 0050)
7. World Saxophone Quartet (*Steppin',* Black Saint BSR 0027)
8. Cecil Taylor (*Silent Tongues,* Arista/Freedom AL 1005)

Appendixes

Symbol(s)	Numbers in Major Scale	Chord Type	Pitches of Chord Built on C
Maj. 7, △7, M7	1–3–5–7	major seventh chord	C–E–G–B
7	1–3–5–♭7	dominant seventh chord	C–E–G–B♭
m7, −7, min. 7	1–♭3–5–♭7	minor seventh chord	C–E♭–G–B♭
ø7	1–♭3–♭5–♭7	half-diminished seventh chord	C–E♭–G♭–B♭
°7	1–♭3–♭5–♭♭7	diminished seventh chord	C–E♭–G♭–B♭♭
+, aug.	1–3–♯5	augmented chord	C–E–G♯
7 sus. 4	1–4–♭7	quartal dominant seventh chord	C–F–B♭

Appendix II
Cassette Tape

Appendix III (pp. 197–200)

Cut Nos.	A. Melodic Dictation (skips of M3 and P4)
#1	1
#2	2
#3	3
#4	4
#5	Interval Dictation 1

	B. Melodic Dictation (skips of tritone and M6)
#6	1
#7	2
#8	3
#9	Interval Dictation 2

	C. Melodic Dictation (skips of m3, m6, and M7)
#10	1
#11	2
#12	3
#13	Interval Dictation 3

	D. Melodic Dictation (skips of m7 and P5)
#14	1
#15	2
#16	3
#17	Interval Dictation 4

Appendix IV (pp. 201–14)

Cut Nos.		ii–V–I Progressions
#18	1.	quartet
#19	2.	trio*
		ii–V Progressions
#20	1.	ii–V descending M2
#21	2.	ii–V ascending M2
#22	3.	ii–V descending m2
#23	4.	ii–V ascending m2
#24	5.	ii–V descending m3
#25	6.	ii–V ascending m3
#26	7.	ii–V descending M3
#27	8.	ii–V ascending M3
#28	9.	ii–V ascending P4
#29	10.	ii–V ascending P5

Appendix V (pp. 215–18)

Cut Nos.	The Blues
	1. Twelve-bar blues in all keys, by ascending half steps
#30	(a) quartet
#31	(b) trio
#32	2. Alternate progression: "Wildwoman Blues"
	3. Alternate blues progressions
#33	(a) 1
#34	(b) 2
#35	(c) 3
#36	(d) 4

*Melodies (pp. 203-4) to be played with recording

Appendix III
Melodic and Intervallic Dictation

From accompanying cassette recording
Melodic Dictation A, B, C, and D.   First pitch is given. Each
    example is repeated. Notate the melodic line.
Interval Dictation 1, 2, 3, and 4.   First pitch of interval is given.
    Possible interval distance is given at beginning of the example.
    Intervals may be ascending or descending. Notate pitch with
    appropriate duration (rest) to fill the measure within each bracket.

A. Melodic Dictation (skips of M3 or P4)

Interval Dictation 1 (M3/P4)

Notate a pitch of correct duration that corresponds to one of the M3/P4 intervals.

B. Melodic Dictation (skips of T or M6)

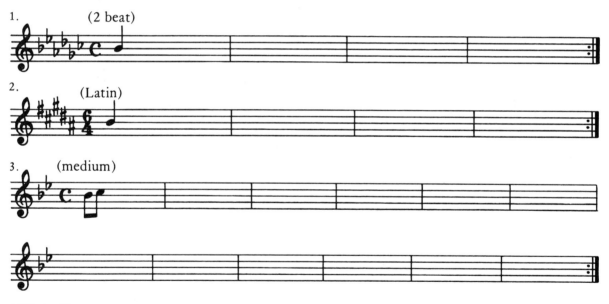

Interval Dictation 2 (T/M6)

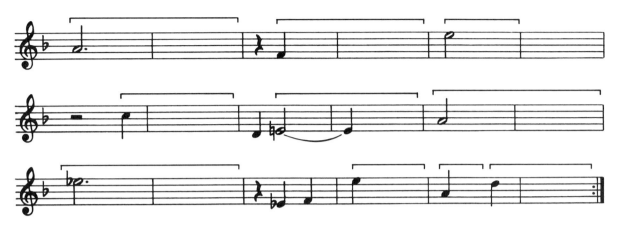

C. Melodic Dictation (skips of m3, m6, M7)

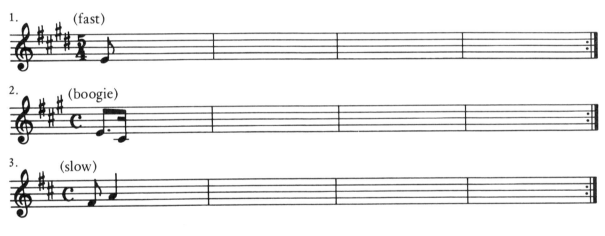

Interval Dictation 3 (m3/m6/M7)

D. Melodic Dictation (skips of m7 or P5)

Interval Dictation 4 (m7/P5/m2/M2/P4)

Appendix IV
Progressions (ii–V–I and ii–V)

*Play over the rhythm section track of ii–V–I

A. ii–V–I Progressions
(twice around the Circle of Fourths)

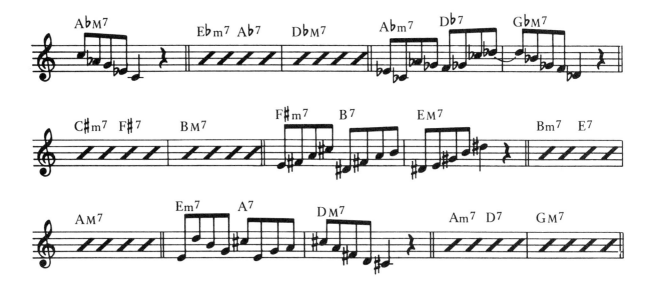

ii–V–I Progressions

Play each of the melodies below around the Circle using the ii–V–I cassette recording. Watch the articulations.

Additional ii–V–I Progressions

B. ii–V Progressions
(from all possible root relationships)

1. ii–V relationship by descending M2
(melodic line over progression by descending M3)

2. ii–V relationship by ascending M2
(melodic line over progression by ascending M3)

3. ii–V relationship by descending m2
(melodic line over progression by descending M2)

4. ii–V relationship by ascending m2
(melodic line over progression by ascending M2)

5. ii–V relationship by descending m3
(melodic line over progression by tritone)

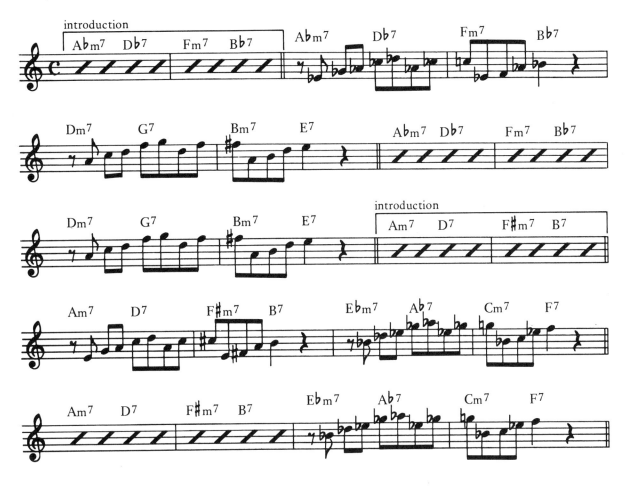

6. ii–V relationship by ascending m3
(melodic line over progression by tritone)

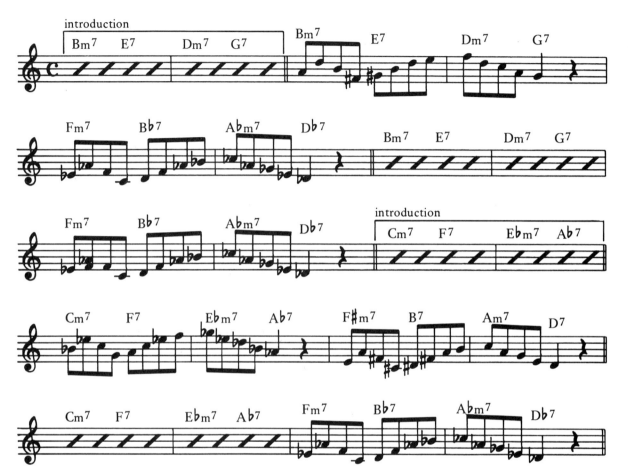

7. ii–V relationship by descending M3
   ## (melodic line over progression by ascending M3)

8. ii–V relationship by ascending M3
(melodic line over progression by descending M3)

9. ii–V relationship by ascending P4
(melodic line over progression by descending M2)

10. ii–V relationship by ascending P5
(melodic line by ascending M2)

Appendix V
The Blues

1. Twelve-bar blues, all keys, by ascending half steps

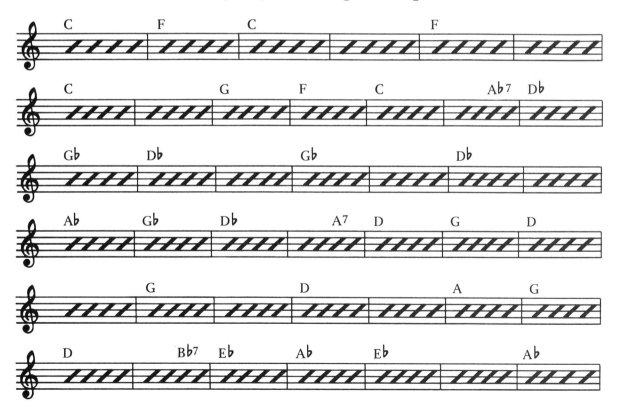

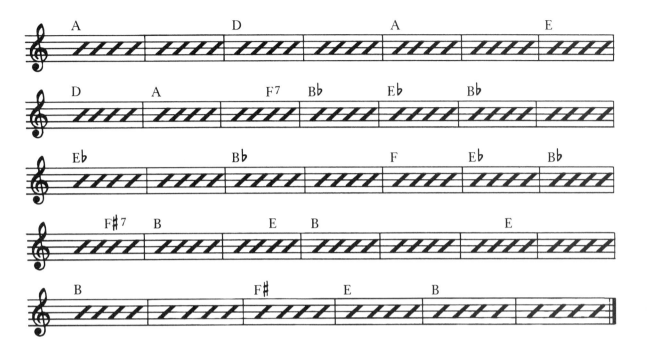

2. "Wildwoman Blues" by Joan Wildman

[3 times]

3. Alternate blues progressions

Appendix VI
Solo Construction

Preparation

Know the composition: (a) memorize the melody and the chord changes; (b) play in several different tempos; (c) measure the relative importance of all transitory keys; (d) assemble possible substitutions, additions, or alterations in the harmony; (e) provide melodic ornamentation, transposition, rhythmic displacement, etc., in the original line.

Know its performance history: (a) who wrote it? (b) when? (c) who has recorded it? (d) what different performance styles are represented in the recordings?

Know which specific qualities of the composition separate it from all others: (a) melodic intervals? (b) harmonic progressions? (c) rhythmic structure? (d) form?

Know which qualities of the composition are most congenial to you so as to enhance your own personal statement about the material.

Performance

Each phrase must sound coherent: (a) build toward a tension peak within each phrase; (b) "finish" each phrase.

Use silence effectively: (a) separate the first motive from the second within a phrase; (b) separate one phrase from another.

Phrases must relate to one another: (a) build toward the climax of a section by a succession of phrases of increasingly high tension peaks; (b) vary phrase lengths; (c) begin the next phrase at a *different* beat of the measure.

The solo must have an overall shape of its own: (a) continue the relationships described above to formulate the tension-and-relaxation shapes of the entire solo. (A solo can be equally interesting whether it contains *one* climactic point somewhere in the middle or several peaks gradually building toward the end); (b) experiment with different solo shapes.

Glossary

addition   improvisation in which additional material is added to original material

alteration   improvisation in which melody, harmony, and/or rhythm are altered

articulation   a combination of phrasing, dynamics, and durational considerations

asymmetrical   not symmetrical, unbalanced

blue notes   originally the flat third and seventh of a major scale, but includes others such as the flat fifth and second

blues   a song of black American origin, marked by use of blue notes: form is usually a twelve-bar chorus consisting of a three-line stanza—with the second line repeating the first

call-and-response   a phrase of music (call), which is then answered (response)

canon   a melody repeated in successive voices

circle of fourths   chord roots or keys an ascending perfect fourth apart—C to F to B♭, etc.

circle progression   refers to the circle of ascending perfect fourths

circularity   melodic repetition that reduces or eliminates tonality

common tones   pitches common to (the same as) adjacent chords

comp   accompany

eleventh chord   a chord consisting of six factors, each a third apart (e.g., F–A–C–E–G–B)

extension   improvisation in which certain melodic or harmonic ideas are extended

harmonic rhythm   the rhythm produced by changes of harmony

head   beginning of a composition

hexachord   a six-note scale

Lydian dominant   addition of a raised fourth scale step to the Mixolydian mode

motif   same as motive

motive   a group (two to ten) of pitches that recur often in a composition

ninth chord   a chord consisting of five factors, each a third apart

nonchord tone   tones not a part of existing harmony; nonharmonic tones

ornamentation   the process of adding new material to decorate the given melodic line

pedal tone   a tone sustained in one voice—others move without reference to it

pentachord   a five-note scale

period   usually a combination of two phrases to form a complete section

phrase   a section of music (usually four or eight measures) ending in a cadence

phrase member   a portion or distinct section (often half) of a phrase

polychords   one (or more) chords superimposed upon another (e.g., C–E–G and F♯–A♯–C♯)

quartal harmony   chords arranged in ascending fourths—rather than in traditional thirds

rhythmic displacement   accents and/or meter are changed, added to, or diminished in value

riff   repeated motives—short group of notes repeated frequently

scale, diminished   a scale in which alternate pitches spell a diminished seventh chord

scale, Dorian   a seven-tone scale with half steps at 2–3 and 6–7

scale, harmonic minor   a seven-tone scale with half steps at 2–3, 5–6, and 7–8

scale, Locrian   a seven-tone scale with half steps at 1–2 and 4–5

scale, Lydian   a seven-tone scale with half steps at 4–5 and 7–8 or 1

scale, major   a seven-tone scale with half steps between 3–4 and 7–8 or 1

scale, melodic minor   a seven tone scale with half steps at 2–3 and 7–8

scale, Mixolydian   a seven-tone scale with half steps at 3–4 and 6–7

scale, natural minor   a seven-tone scale with half steps at 2–3 and 5–6

scale, pentatonic   a five-tone scale

scale, Phrygian   a seven-tone scale with half steps at 1–2 and 5–6

sequence   the immediate restating of a melodic figure at a higher or lower pitch

substitution   different material is substituted for the original

temporary tonic   usually the traditional resolution of a secondary dominant (tonicized)

tension-relaxation   a movement from tension or unrest to relaxation (repose or rest)

tetrachord   a series of four pitches consisting of adjacent alphabetical letters

thirteenth chord   a chord consisting of seven factors, each a third apart (e.g., F–A–C–E–G–B–D)

transitory key   temporary key or hint of a tonal center, such as a secondary dominant

traveling chords   chords moving toward the tonic, frequently secondary dominants

trichord   any combination of three pitches

tritone   augmented fourth or diminished fifth

voicing   the vertical arrangement of pitches in a chord

Index